Prayers & Meditations for Friday Evening
Jewish Religious Writings

with Gender-Neutral & All-Embracing
Translation & Commentary

Edited by
H. G. Gerjuoy

Graphic Design – Judi Ann Goodman

Jaelle Publishing

© 2015 H. G. Gerjuoy

In memory of my daughter, Judith Hope Gerjuoy – יְהוּדִית תִּקְוָה (1955-2013), an אֵשֶׁת־חַיִל.

This prayer and meditation book may be used by an individual or by a congregation. It contains –

- Titles, e.g., **Lighting the Sabbath Candles**
- Directions to the congregation, e.g., PLEASE RISE.
- Hebrew or Aramaic, e.g., וְאָהַבְתָּ
- English alphabet transliteration of the Hebrew or Aramaic, e.g., *v'-a-**ha**-v'-ta*. Spaces between table columns, or "< >"s, indicate recitation pauses.

    transliteration pronunciation guide:

    - ʼ   the schwa: a brief and faint, or very brief and very faint, neutral vowel
    - *a* – like "ah", but may be shorter
    - *ai* – like "eye"
    - *aw* – like "aw" in "shawl"
    - *ay* – like "ay" in "say"
    - *e* – like "e" in "bet"
    - *ee* – like "ee" in "see", but may be shorter
    - *g* - always hard, as in "go"
    - *i* – like "i" in "pin"
    - *kh* – like "ch" in German "ach" or Scotch "loch"
    - *o* – like "o" in "go", but may be shorter
    - *u* – like "oo" in "book" or like "oo" in "toot", but may be shorter
    - \- separates syllables, e.g., *l'-sha-**bay**-akh*

    Other English alphabet letters or letter pairs, namely, *b, d, f, h, j, k, l, m, n, p, r, s, t, v, w, z, oy*, and *sh* are pronounced as they commonly are in English.

    Hebrew accent or stress is usually on the last syllable; when not, it is sometimes indicated by boldface, e.g., *v'-a-**ha**-v'-ta*

- Literal or almost literal word by word English translation of the Hebrew or Aramaic, e.g., **And you shall love**.

    English and Hebrew words do not correspond word for word. Moreover, even when English and Hebrew words have roughly the same meaning, their connotations often differ. Furthermore, English and Hebrew grammars call attention to or tend to obscure different dimensions of meaning. Therefore, there is usually no one exact English translation of a Hebrew passage. I have had to make choices, and alternative "literal" translations are often justifiable. Occasionally, I provide alternative translations separated by "\"; a multi-word alternative is in square brackets ("[" . . ."]").

- More penetrating, expressive, free, or poetic English rendering of the Hebrew, revealing some of the deeper meanings or allusions, e.g., Lovingly obey. (The same font is used for comments or meditation selections.) The word by word translations may help the reader understand the sources of the less literal translations.

    In these renderings, the English sometimes parallels the Hebrew pattern of syllables, stresses, or rhymes.

    Although Hebrew has been remarkably stable as the millennia have passed, some words' denotations or connotations have changed. Occasionally, my free English rendering reflects meaning that has evolved since the passage originated.

    Unlike English, regardless whether the user wishes to call attention to gender, nearly all Hebrew words are explicitly feminine or masculine. Except where I felt that the meaning of the Hebrew required gender be explicit, I have chosen gender-neutral English translations. For example, I have used "God" or "Sovereign" where the literal translation might be "He," "King," or "Lord."

- Added or optional content, in curly brackets ("{ . . . }").

- Comments not normally read aloud, e.g., by Rabbi Eliezer Azikri.
    Comments in the Meditation section, pp. 22-50, are not colored.

As illustrated above, the various kinds of content are distinguished by color, font, or being in curly brackets.

Contents

Preface	vii
*Y'-deed **Ne**-fesh*	1-5
Numbers 24:5 (*Ma **to**-vu*)	6
Lighting the Sabbath Candles	7
Welcoming the Sabbath	8-12
Psalm 133:1 (*Hi-nay Ma Tov*)	8
L'-kha Do-dee	9
Song of Songs 1:2-3, 2:16, 3:6, 4:9, 4:16	10-12
Sh'-ma, etc.	13-17
Bless God (*Ba-r'-khu*)	13
Deuteronomy 6:4 (*Sh'-ma*)	14
Deuteronomy 6:5-9 (*V'-a-**ha**-v'-ta*)	15-16
Exodus 15:11 (*Mee kha-**mo**-kha*)	17
Miriam's Song – Exodus 15:20-21	18
The *A-mee-da* (Standing) Prayer	19-21
Psalm 51:15	19
Ancestors	19
Sabbath	20
Exodus 31:16	20
Grant Peace	20
Meditation	22-50
Psalm 92	22-25
Anything May Be Prayer If the Intent Is To Pray	26
Eternal God	27
Little Muttle's Prayer	28
Psalm 97	29-30
Psalm 121	31-32
The Eight Degrees of Charity	33
Psalm 19:1-10	34-36
Ts'daka [Charity] in Our Lives	37
Judaism's Tradition of Commentary and Debate	38

Contents Cont.

Prayer Is Not Enough: We Must Also Act	39
Maimonides's Thirteen Principles of Jewish Faith	40
Isaiah 1:11-17	41
Micah 6:8	42
Isaiah 42:1-7	42-43
Isaiah 56: 1-7	43-44
Amos 5:24	44
What Is Holy?	45
Proverbs 31:10-31	46-49
Ecclesiastes Rabbah (Haggadic Commentary) 7:13	50
After the *A-mee-da* (Standing) Prayer and Meditation	51
Psalm 19:15	51
O-se Sha-lom	51
The Soul Is Pure	52
It Is Up To Us	53-55
Isaiah 2:4	56-57
Memorial (Mourning) Meditation	58
Psalm 144:3-4	58
Psalm 90:6	58
Psalm 90:12	58
The Mourners' Kaddish	59-61
Nothing Is Like Our God	62-63
Yi-g'-dal	64
A-don O-lam	65-67
Psalm 23	68-70
Blessing Children (Numbers 6:24-26)	71
Kiddush – Sanctification	72
Blessing for Wine	73
Blessing for Bread	74
Ha-sh'-kee-vay-nu	75-76
Acknowledgments	77

Preface

As I prepared this book, I tried to picture readers whom I might be addressing. One such is a young adult who feels coerced to attend a prayer service. I hope to provide that reader with content that will help her or him feel that attending the service is not time wasted. Another (or possibly another part of the same) reader is one who has been ill-treated, perhaps because of the reader's gender or gender preference, or perhaps because of some other physical or cultural baggage carried by the reader or others. I hope to point toward a path that moves from blaming to cooperative problem solving, and transcends both rebellion against and submission to coercive authority, offering mutual compassion, forgiveness, reconciliation, release, and understanding to oppressors and oppressed.

Among my attitudes and beliefs reflected, perhaps latently, in this book are:

- humans are naturally cooperative;
- exploitation or slavery is neither desirable nor inevitable;
- expansion of human freedom is desirable;
- no human gender is superior; none should dominate any other;
- governments and society should benefit all, not the strong at the cost of the weak;
- peace is better than war;
- humans should not seek power solely for the sake of power;
- people of all ranks can make valuable contributions to humankind;
- reduction of suffering is desirable;
- mutual trust among individuals and among groups is desirable and learnable;
- humans do not profit solely by forcing others to lose; human interaction is not zero-sum;
- respecting and honoring God, justice, law, and tradition is desirable;
- among virtues are altruism, benevolence, charity, empathy, forgivingness, friendliness, gentleness, good nature, kindness, pity, politeness, public spirit, sympathy, temperance, tolerance, and unselfishness.

About use of the word "God" in this book – Some may object to my use of the word "God" as if it refers to something real. I respond: It is irrelevant whether God exists, what "God" denotes, or even whether the word has denotative meaning. Rabbi Aryeh Kaplan (1934-1983) once remarked to me that whatever we say about God is necessarily wrong. I believe he was referring to the denotative meaning of "God." But "God" has connotative meaning, including connoting mystery (experience that transcends reason or understanding). Statements about God need not satisfy the shibboleths of logical positivism. They may be as revelatory as a Zen koan.

Prayer is not a magic spell – Many believers in magic think its spells work whether or not the reciter or performer understands and means what is said or done. In prayer, conscious intent is essential. If magic were real, one might cast a spell without awareness; one cannot pray without awareness and intent. This is one reason for the English translations of non-English content in this book.

*Y'-deed **Ne**-fesh*

1st Stanza

יְדִיד נֶפֶשׁ, אָב הָרַחֲמָן,
מְשׁוֹךְ עַבְדְּךָ אֶל רְצוֹנָךְ,
יָרוּץ עַבְדְּךָ כְּמוֹ אַיָּל,
יִשְׁתַּחֲוֶה מוּל הֲדָרָךְ.

*Y'-deed **ne**-fesh, av ha-**ra**-kha-man,
M'-shokh a-v'-dakh el r'-tso-nakh.
Ya-ruts a-v'-dakh k'-mo a-yal,
Yi-sh'-**ta**-kha-ve mul ha-da-rakh.*

**Soul-mate, compassionate Parent,
draw Your servant to Your desire.
Your servant will run like a ram,
will bow facing Your way.**

Soul-mate, compassionate Nurturer,
shape me, Your servant, as You desire.
I, Your servant, will rush like a hart
to bow before Your Presence.

כִּי יֶעֱרַב לוֹ יְדִידוּתָךְ
מִנֹּפֶת צוּף וְכָל טָעַם

*kee ye-e-rav lo y'-dee-du-takh,
mi-**no**-fet tsuf v'-khawl **ta**-am.*

**Because Your love for me will be more pleasant
than nectar or any good taste.**

To me, Your love is more delightful
than nectar or any other source of pleasure.

*Y'-deed **Ne**-fesh* Cont.

2nd Stanza

הָדוּר, נָאֶה, זִיו הָעוֹלָם
נַפְשִׁי חוֹלַת אַהֲבָתָךְ
אָנָא, אֵל נָא, רְפָא נָא לָהּ
בְּהַרְאוֹת לָהּ נֹעַם זִיוָךְ
אָז תִּתְחַזֵּק וְתִתְרַפֵּא,
וְהָיְתָה לָךְ שִׁפְחַת עוֹלָם

*Ha-dur, na-e, zeev ha-o-lam,
na-f'-shee <u>kh</u>o-lat a-ha-va-ta<u>kh</u>,
a-na, Ayl na, r'-fa na la,
b'-ha-r'-ot la **no**-am zee-va<u>kh</u>
az ti-t'-<u>kh</u>a-zayk v'-ti-t'-ra-pay,
v'-ha-y'-ta la<u>kh</u> si-f'-<u>kh</u>at o-lam.*

**Splendid\illustrious\elegant, pleasant\fine, Radiance\
Brightness\Brilliance of the world\universe,
my soul is sick for love of You.
Please, God, please cure her, please,
by revealing, please, the pleasantness of
Your radiance\brightness\brilliance.
Then You will strengthen and heal,
and there will be for her eternal bliss.**

Glorious One, how beautifully You light up the universe!
My soul is sick with love for You.
Please, God, please heal my soul, please,
by revealing Your exquisite radiance.
Then my soul will be invigorated and healed
and will experience everlasting bliss.

*Y'-deed **Ne**-fesh* Cont.

3rd Stanza

וָתִיק, יֶהֱמוּ רַחֲמֶיךָ,
וְחוּס נָא עַל בֵּן אוֹהֲבָךְ
כִּי זֶה כַּמֶּה נִכְסֹף נִכְסַף
לִרְאוֹת מְהֵרָה בְּתִפְאֶרֶת עֻזָּךְ
אָנָא, אֵלִי, מַחְמַד לִבִּי,
חוּשָׁה נָּא, וְאַל תִּתְעַלָּם.

*Va-teek, ye-h'-mu ra-<u>kh</u>a-**may**-<u>kh</u>a,*
v'-<u>kh</u>us na al bayn o-ha-va<u>kh</u>
kee ze ka-me ni-<u>kh</u>'-sof ni-<u>kh</u>'-saf
*li-r'-ot m'-hay-ra b'-ti-f'-**e**-ret u-za<u>kh</u>*
a-na, Ay-lee, ma-<u>kh</u>'-mad li-bee,
<u>kh</u>u-sha na, v'-al ti-t'-a-lam.

O Senior One, please, may Your mercy be aroused,
and please be gracious to Your beloved child,
for this is how much I long, I yearn
to see soon the splendor of Your might.
Please, my God, my heart's delight,
please empathize and do not hide.

Please, O Ancient One, may Your mercy be stirred,
and please be generous to Your beloved child,
for I have yearned and yearned to witness promptly your sublime splendor.
Please, my God, my heart's desire,
please sense my craving and do not conceal Yourself.

*Y'-deed **Ne**-fesh* Cont.

4th Stanza

הִגָּלֵה נָא וּפְרוֹשׂ חָבִיב עָלַי
אֶת סֻכַּת שְׁלוֹמָךְ
תָּאִיר אֶרֶץ מִכְּבוֹדֶךָ,
נָגִילָה וְנִשְׂמְחָה בָךְ
מַהֵר, אָהוּב, כִּי בָא מוֹעֵד
וְחָנֵנוּ כִּימֵי עוֹלָם

*Hi-ga-lay na u-f'-ros kha-veev a-lai,
et su-kat sh'-lo-makh
ta-eer e-rets mi-k'-vo-d'-kha,
na-gee-la v'-ni-s'-m'-kha vakh
ma-hayr, A-huv, kee va mo-ayd
v'-kha-nay-nu kee-may o-lam.*

**Please be visible, and over me spread the pleasantness
of the shelter of Your peace.
Light up the earth with Your honor\respect.
We will rejoice and be happy about You.
Hurry, Darling, because the time is come,
and be gracious to us as in olden times.**

Reveal Yourself and spread over me the delightful pleasure
of the shelter of Your peace.
Light up the earth with Your glory!
We will rejoice and be happy about You.
Hurry, Darling, for the time is coming!
And be gracious to us as in olden times.

*Y'-deed **Ne-fesh** Cont.*

Y'-deed Ne-fesh is probably by the 16-17th-century(?) kabbalist, Rabbi Eliezer Azikri of Safed. The initial letters of the Hebrew stanzas spell the Tetragrammaton name of God. The genders of both God and the poet differ in different early texts.

Expanding on the start of Psalm 42, it is a passionate expression of unconditional love for and submission to God. Throughout history, absolute dictators have required similar outpourings from their subjects. The stars of such "cults of personality" demand from their subjects absolute unquestioning fealty; they acknowledge no higher power. They either explicitly claim to be divine or attribute to themselves godlike powers. Recent examples include Hitler, Stalin, and any number of contemporary despots. We may speculate that unquestioning obedience to a human leader's commands evolved to ensure that members of a primitive tribe would cooperate and act in coordination, even when this entailed sacrifice by individuals. In classical times, the Israelites were exceptions to such slavishness. The prophets of Israel proclaimed that even the king must submit to God, that a ruler's commands were to be obeyed only when they did not transgress God's commandments. Indeed, because the Israelites considered only God deserving of obeisance, they refused to bow to any human. This was among the reasons conquerors of Israel ruthlessly oppressed the Israelites.

Perhaps, when the Israelites replaced submission to human rulers with fealty to an invisible universal God, this freed them, rather than diminished their freedom.

Of course, submission to God's commands could only be fully freeing if interpreters of God's commands were limited in what they could require in God's name. Otherwise, absolute priests or prophets would have replaced absolute kings. Submission to God helps immunize us from submission to human dictators only when we have a body of Law, a Torah, that limits what a human may demand in God's name. However, a fixed body of Law could have become a straightjacket, preventing us from adapting over the centuries to changing times and circumstances. Therefore, we have a tradition of cautiously and respectfully consensually reinterpreting without changing the Torah. Century after century, Judaism has paradoxically counterpoised tradition and reinterpretation. Thus, Judaism has survived, offering freedom from submission to tyrants, a body of age-old commandments, and a process for reinterpreting those commandments to meet new challenges.

Numbers 24:5

מַה־טֹּבוּ אֹהָלֶיךָ, יַעֲקֹב, מִשְׁכְּנֹתֶיךָ, יִשְׂרָאֵל!

*Ma **to**-vu o-ha-**lay**-<u>kha</u>, Ya-a-kov, mi-sh'-k'-no-**tay**-<u>kha</u>, Yi-s'-ra-ayl!*

How good your tents are, Jacob, your residences, Israel!

How fine your tents are, Jacob, your sanctuaries, Israel!

In Numbers, we learn that Balak, king of Moab, fearing the might of the Israelites, asked the pagan prophet, Balaam, to curse the Israelites. Balaam, inspired by God, blessed them instead, saying the words above. Our custom is to say these words when entering a house of Jewish worship, a synagogue.

It is interesting that Divine inspiration is not an exclusively Israelite capacity.

מַה־טֹּבוּ אֹהָלַיִךְ, שָׂרָה, מִשְׁכְּנֹתַיִךְ, רִבְקָה!

*Ma **to**-vu o-ha-**la**-yi<u>kh</u>, Sa-ra, mi-sh'-k'-no-**ta**-yi<u>kh</u>, Ri-v'-ka!*

How good your tents are, Sarah, your residences, Rebecca!

How fine your tents are, Sarah, your sanctuaries, Rebecca!

Lighting the Sabbath Candles

בָּרוּךְ אַתָּה, יְיָ* אֱלֹהֵינוּ, מֶלֶךְ הָעוֹלָם, אֲשֶׁר קִדְּשָׁנוּ בְּמִצְוֹתָיו וְצִוָּנוּ לְהַדְלִיק נֵר שֶׁל־שַׁבָּת.

*Ba-ru<u>kh</u> A-ta, A-do-nai E-lo-**hay**-nu, **Me**-le<u>kh</u> ha-o-lam, a-sher ki-d'-**sha**-nu b'-mi-ts'-vo-taiv v'-tsi-**va**-nu l'-ha-d'-leek nayr shel sha-bat.*

Bless You, [Eternal One]\[Who was, is, and will be], our God, Ruler of the world\universe\multiverse, Whose commandments have made us holy and Who commanded us to light Sabbath candles.

Blessed is the Eternal Who inspires us to kindle the Sabbath lights; blessed is the Source of life and light.

Sabbath is the day of celebration of life in its deepest sense: creation. Beginning with celebration of light, we take a moment to light two candles: one for the light within, the other for what we share with others.

May the brightness of these candles banish all gloom, anxiety, and care from my heart and from the hearts of my loved ones.

May this Sabbath bring us peace and serenity, joy and rest. May it keep aglow within us the spirit of gratitude for Your many blessings, so that we may know the sweet taste of contentment and the rich harvest of sharing.

Kindle in our homes a deeper love for one another, for our people, and for all Your children.

Based on material in United Nation Environment Programme, *Only One Earth.* United Nations, NY: 1990.

---

*"יְיָ," which may be pronounced "*A-do-nai*," is in this book where the not-to-be-pronounced Tetragrammaton, "יהוה", might appear. There are many mystical interpretations of the Tetragrammaton. A non-mystical one: it is an abbreviation of "הָיָה, הֹוֶה, יְהְיֶה" – "**was, is, will be**". Since ancient times, Hebrew usage has avoided these verb forms, which might be "in vain" references to God.

Welcoming the Sabbath

Psalm 133: 1

הִנֵּה מַה־טּוֹב וּמַה־נָּעִים　　שֶׁבֶת אַחִים גַּם־יָחַד:

Hi-nay ma tov u-ma na-eem　　*she-vet a-kheem gam ya-khad.*

Behold how good and how pleasant　　**living\sitting brothers also\even together.**

See how good and pleasant:　　brothers and sisters companions together.

Traditionally, the Sabbath is when we let go our weekday burdens and struggles, and our spirits are renewed. The traditional metaphor for this is that we acquire an additional soul. During the Sabbath, by tradition we do things we lack time for during the week, such as doing nothing, reading, meditating, or group singing. The songs express our dreams and our joy in life and community.

L'-kha Do-dee

לְכָה דוֹדִי לִקְרַאת כַּלָּה   פְּנֵי שַׁבָּת נְקַבְּלָה
בּוֹאִי בְשָׁלוֹם עֲטֶרֶת בַּעְלָהּ   גַּם בְּשִׂמְחָה וּבְצָהֳלָה

L'-*kha* Do-dee li-k'-rat ka-la.   p'-nay sha-bat n'-ka-b'-la.

Bo-ee v'-sha-lom a-**te**-ret ba-'-la.   gam b'-si-m'-*kha* u-v'-tsa-ha-la.

Let's Go, My Love

Let's go, my love, toward the bride; we'll receive\welcome\greet the Sabbath. Come in peace, your Sovereign's diadem, with festivity and shouts of joy.

L'-kha Do-dee was written by Rabbi Solomon haLevi Alkabetz, a sixteenth century Safed kabbalist. Of its ten stanzas, above are the introductory first and part of the last. Traditionally, before the last stanza, to welcome the arrival of the Sabbath bride-queen, the congregants rise, face the door, and bow.

Song of Songs, 1:2-3

יִשָּׁקֵנִי מִנְּשִׁיקוֹת פִּיהוּ,
כִּי־טוֹבִים דֹּדֶיךָ מִיָּיִן.
לְרֵיחַ שְׁמָנֶיךָ טוֹבִים,

*Yi-sha-**kay**-nee mi-n'-shee-kot **pee**-hoo,*
*Kee to-veem do-**day**-<u>kh</u>a mee-**ya**-yin.*
*L'-**ray**-a<u>kh</u> sh'-ma-**nay**-<u>kh</u>a to-veem,*

Let him kiss me with the kisses of his mouth,
For your love is better than wine.
Your ointments' fragrances are good.

The Song of Songs is a collection of romantic and sometimes quite sensual or erotic verses. Traditionally, they have been portrayed as expressing romantic and passionate love of God, like the expressions in *Y'-deed **Ne**-fesh*. Traditionally, the Song of Songs is recited during the Orthodox Friday evening service. After the service, when permitted by the commandments that pertain to such activity, love-making by married couples is traditionally encouraged.

Zoroastreanism, Manichaeanism, and religions they influenced regard the body and its pleasures as creations of a rival to God, and hence inherently evil. Strictly monotheistic Judaism regards body and spirit as dual aspects of one creation by the one and only God, and so considers erotic pleasure, in an appropriate setting, to be a holy blessing.

Jewish mystics sometimes wrote אתבש - **azbyically** -coded texts, interchanging א and ת, ב and ש, etc. They also sometimes used the first letters of successive words to spell an allied message. The English below may suggest how the latter worked.

Lust **e**xquisitely **t**riumphing, **h**e **i**s **m**e, **k**issed **i**nto **s**uch **s**weetness, **m**y **e**agerness, **w**armed **i**nto **t**rue **h**eat, **t**he **h**eat **e**ntrancing, **k**issing **i**n **s**uch **s**weetness **e**ach **s**welling, **o**r **f**ever, **h**eated **i**nto **s**urging, **m**ore **o**rganically **u**rgent **t**han **h**eat. **F**eelings **o**f **r**apture, **t**hey **h**eal **y**ou, **l**eaps **o**f **v**irile **e**nthusiasm, **i**nside **s**weetness, **b**eyond **e**uphoria **t**enderly **t**ouching **e**ach **r**apture, **t**wice **h**ere **a**nd **n**ow, **w**arming **i**nto **n**ew **e**cstasy. **T**hus **h**e **i**s **n**ow **e**ntered, **o**r **i**s **n**ow **t**he **m**oment **e**ach **n**ew **t**ouch **s**eems, **h**ardly **a** **v**irginal **e**cho, **a**zbyically, **g**host **o**f **o**ld **d**esire **l**oving **y**ou, **f**or **r**emembered **a**gonies **g**rown **r**apturous **a**nd **n**ow **c**limaxing **e**cstatically? . . .

Song of Songs, 2:16, 3:6, 4:9, 4:16 adapted.

דּוֹדִי לִי

דּוֹדִי לִי, וַאֲנִי לוֹ, הָרֹעֶה בַּשׁוֹשַׁנִּים.

מִי זֹאת עֹלָה מִן־הַמִּדְבָּר?
מִי זֹאת עֹלָה
מְקֻטֶּרֶת מֹר, מֹר וּלְבוֹנָה,
מֹר וּלְבוֹנָה?
דּוֹדִי לִי, וַאֲנִי לוֹ, הָרֹעֶה בַּשׁוֹשַׁנִּים.

לִבַּבְתִּנִי אֲחֹתִי כַלָּה; לִבַּבְתִּנִי כַלָּה!

דּוֹדִי לִי, וַאֲנִי לוֹ, הָרֹעֶה בַּשׁוֹשַׁנִּים.

עוּרִי צָפוֹן! וּבוֹאִי תֵימָן!

דּוֹדִי לִי, וַאֲנִי לוֹ, הָרֹעֶה בַּשׁוֹשַׁנִּים.
דּוֹדִי לִי, וַאֲנִי לוֹ, הָרֹעֶה בַּשׁוֹשַׁנִּים.

Song of Songs, 2:16, 3:6, 4:9, 4:16 adapted Cont.

Do-dee lee, va-a-nee lo, ha-ro-e ba-sho-sha-neem.

Mee zot o-la min ha-mi-d'-bar?
Mee zot o-la
*M'-ku-**te**-ret mor, mor u-l'-vo-na,*
Mor u-l'-vo-na?
Do-dee lee, va-a-nee lo, ha-ro-e ba-sho-sha-neem.

*Li-ba-v'-**ti**-nee a-<u>kh</u>o-tee <u>kh</u>a-la; li-ba-v'-**ti**-nee <u>kh</u>a-la!*

Do-dee lee, va-a-nee lo, ha-ro-e ba-sho-sha-neem.

*U-ree tsa-fon! U-**vo**-ee tay-man!*

Twice: *Do-dee lee, va-a-nee lo, ha-ro-e ba-sho-sha-neem.*

My Love Is Mine

"My love is mine and I am his, he who is a shepherd among the roses."

"Who is she who is coming up from the wilderness?
"Who is she who is coming up
"perfumed with myrrh and frankincense,
"myrrh and frankincense?"
"My love is mine, and I am his, he who is a shepherd among the roses."

"My sweetheart, my sister bride, my sweetheart bride!"

"My love is mine, and I am his, he who is a shepherd among the roses."

"Wake up, North\[hidden one]! And come, South!"

Twice: **"My love is mine, and I am his, he who is a shepherd among the roses."**

Sh'-ma Service

Bless God

CONGREGANTS: PLEASE RISE.

בָּרְכוּ אֶת־יְיָ הַמְבֹרָךְ׃

Ba-r'-khu et A-do-nai ha-m'-vo-rakh.

Bless God the bless-worthy.

CONGREGANTS: PLEASE BOW WHILE SAYING THE FOLLOWING.

בָּרוּךְ יְיָ הַמְבֹרָךְ לְעוֹלָם וָעֶד׃

Ba-rukh A-do-nai ha-m'-vo-rakh l'-o-lam va-ed.

Bless God the bless-worthy eternally forever.

CONGREGANTS: YOU MAY BE SEATED.

Deuteronomy 6:4

שְׁמַע יִשְׂרָאֵל יְיָ, אֱלֹהֵינוּ, יְיָ אֶחָד:

Sh'-ma Yi-s'-ra-ayl A-do-nai, E-lo-hay-nu, A-do-nai e-khad.

Listen, Israel, our God\Sovereign, our God is One.

I hereby testify that the Eternal One is our God, that the Eternal One is a Unity.

WHETHER READING INDIVIDUALLY OR IN A GROUP, DIFFERENT READERS MAY SUBSTITUTE ALTERNATIVE EXAMPLES FOR THOSE BELOW IN CURLY BRACKETS.

We reject polytheism –

- For different tribes, nations, or groups of people there is only one God; it is therefore absurd to believe or assert "Our God is more powerful than our enemy's God";
- Because God is outside of space, different geographic locations all have the same God; for example, the God of {Athens} is the same as the God of {Rome} or the God of {Jerusalem} or the God of {Nineveh};
- Different human activities have the same God: The God of {medicine} is the same as the God of {war}, the God of {love}, or the God of {commerce};
- Different aspects of nature have the same God: The {thunderstorm} God is the same as the {ocean} God or the {sun} God.

Because God is outside of time, God does not change. The same God with Whom you are relating right now is simultaneously relating to the Israelites as they escape from Pharaoh.

God has no internal structure, no components, no parts that we can distinguish.

> Traditionally, the ע in the first word and the ד in the last word of the *sh'ma* are emphasized. They spell the Hebrew word for "witness."
>
> Some pray not only with speech but also with their whole bodies, with posture and gesture. Therefore, when they say אֶחָד – *e-khad* – One, they raise an index finger.

Deuteronomy 6:5-9

Mezzuzah case*

וְאָהַבְתָּ אֵת יְיָ אֱלֹהֶיךָ בְּכָל־לְבָבְךָ וּבְכָל־נַפְשְׁךָ
וּבְכָל־מְאֹדֶךָ
וְהָיוּ הַדְּבָרִים הָאֵלֶּה אֲשֶׁר אָנֹכִי מְצַוְּךָ הַיּוֹם עַל־לְבָבֶךָ
וְשִׁנַּנְתָּם לְבָנֶיךָ וְדִבַּרְתָּ בָּם
בְּשִׁבְתְּךָ בְּבֵיתֶךָ וּבְלֶכְתְּךָ בַדֶּרֶךְ וּבְשָׁכְבְּךָ וּבְקוּמֶךָ
וּקְשַׁרְתָּם לְאוֹת עַל־יָדֶךָ וְהָיוּ לְטֹטָפֹת בֵּין עֵינֶיךָ
וּכְתַבְתָּם עַל־מְזֻזוֹת בֵּיתֶךָ וּבִשְׁעָרֶיךָ

V'-a-ha-v'-ta ayt A-do-nai E-lo-**hay**-<u>kh</u>a b'-<u>kh</u>awl l'-**va**-v'-<u>kh</u>a u-v'-<u>kh</u>awl na-f'-sh'-<u>kh</u>a
u-v'-<u>kh</u>awl m'-o-**de**-<u>kh</u>a.
V'-ha-yu ha-d'-va-reem ha-**ay**-le a-sher **A**-no-<u>kh</u>ee m'-tsa-v'-<u>kh</u>a ha-yom al l'-va-**ve**-<u>kh</u>a.
V'-shi-na-n'-tam l'-va-**nay**-<u>kh</u>a v'-di-ba-r'-ta bam
b'-shi-v'-t'-<u>kh</u>a b'-vay-**te**-<u>kh</u>a u-v'-le-<u>kh</u>'-t'-<u>kh</u>a va-**de**-re<u>kh</u> u-v'-sha-<u>kh</u>'-b'-<u>kh</u>a
u-v'-ku-**me**-<u>kh</u>a.
U-k'-sha-r'-tam l'-ot al ya-**de**-<u>kh</u>a v'-ha-yu l'-**to**-ta-fot bayn ay-**nay**-<u>kh</u>a.
U-<u>kh</u>'-ta-v'-tam al m'-zu-zot bay-**te**-<u>kh</u>a u-vi-sh'-a-**ray**-<u>kh</u>a

And you should love the Lord your God with all your heart and with all your soul and with all your might.
And these words, which I am commanding you today, should be on your heart.
Teach them precisely\penetratingly\fluently to your children, and talk about them
when you are sitting in your house, and when you are walking on the road, and when you lie down, and when you get up.
And you shall tie them on your hand as a sign, and they shall be fastened between your eyes.
And you shall write them on the doorposts of your houses and on your gates.

---

*commons.wikimedia.org/wiki/File:Mezzuzah.1.jpg/ Public Domain

Deuteronomy 6:5-9 Cont.

Some touch their chests near their hearts when they say לְבָבְךָ [*l'-va-v'-kha*] or לְבָבֶךָ [*l'-va-ve-kha*] [your heart], left arms near the biceps when they say יָדֶךָ [*ya-de-kha*] [your arm], and foreheads near the "third eye" when they say בֵּין עֵינֶיךָ [*bayn ay-nay-kha*] [between your eyes].

Lovingly subscribe wholeheartedly to My purposes implied by My commandments, regardless what it may cost you, even if you risk your life by doing so, for this is how to become intimate with Me. My commandments should always be fresh and vivid in your mind, dominating your attention, impossible to ignore. You should never feel, "Oh, I know that already; there is nothing new here that I have to focus on." These words should always be on the tip of your tongue. You should pass them on as if you were a sage instructing disciples. You should give them the highest priority in your actions and in your conversations, whatever the circumstances or time of day or night. Write them on a parchment scroll inside a phylactery you place on your left arm and inside another centered on your forehead. Spread the word when you are in a public place, even in a foreign land.

Partly based on commentary by Rabbi Solomon bar Isaac ("Rashi"), 1040-1105

Exodus 15:11

מִי־כָמֹכָה בָּאֵלִים יְיָ,
מִי כָּמֹכָה נֶאְדָּר בַּקֹּדֶשׁ,
נוֹרָא תְהִלֹּת, עֹשֵׂה־פֶלֶא:

Mee kha-mo-kha ba-ay-leem A-do-nai?
Mee ka-mo-kha ne-'-dar ba-ko-desh,
No-ra t'-hi-lot, o-say fe-le?

Who is like You among the transcendent beings, God?
Who is like You, resplendent in holiness,
Awesomely praised, doing wonders?

Who among the mighty can compare with You, Lord?
Who can compare with You, resplendent in holiness, doing marvels?

Because the praise You deserve transcends what language can express, when we praise You, we fear that our praise is insufficient.

Based on commentary by Rashi.

Miriam's Song

Our *Mee kha-mo-kha* prayer is part of Moses' song (Exodus 15:1-19) celebrating the Israelites' successful crossing of the Red Sea and the drowning of Pharaoh's army. The very next Torah passage is Miriam's song (Exodus 15:20-21):

Then Miriam, the prophet, Aaron's sister, took the tambourine in her hand, and all the women went out after her with tambourines and with circle dancing. And Miriam led them [men and women], chanting: "Sing to the Lord, for He has overwhelmingly overcome! He has cast horse and rider into the sea."

Much of the Torah focuses on men's initiatives. We might believe, consequently, that traditional Judaism did not respect women's initiatives. However, according to Dr. Gabriel Hayyim Cohn, Professor of Bible Studies, Bar-Ilan University, the Torah passage about Miriam's song demonstrates that a woman's initiative was not merely tolerated: it was a major event in the evolution of Judaism. Professor Cohn points out that Miriam, by introducing musical instruments and dance, added a creative artistic dimension to the thanksgiving initiated by Moses, thus deepening and rendering more multi-faceted the spiritual experience.

Sarah Yehudit Schneider, Founder-Director of "A Still Small Voice," an Orthodox correspondence school based in Jerusalem, cites commentary by Rabbi Kalonymus Kalman HaLevi Epstein (1751(?)-1823) of Cracow. Rabbi Epstein notes that Moses and Miriam began their public thanksgiving differently. Moses started, "I will sing," stating a fact about what he, alone, was about to do, while Miriam began by calling on the congregation to join with her. Moses' approach reflects a hierarchical viewpoint in which he separates himself from and places himself ahead of his congregation, while Miriam's is non-hierarchical. That she leads a circle dance rather than a line dance is emblematic of this egalitarian view.

According to Schneider, Rabbi Epstein explains that the Kabbalah considers the male role to be bestowal, and the female to be reception. Thus, teachers are masculine in relation to their pupils. However, in the Messianic era, when all humans will have attained enlightenment, "all power disparities will cease, including the archetypal source of them all, the hierarchy of gender, with its asymmetrical distribution of authority and dependency." Just as all points on a circle are equidistant from its center, so, in the Messianic era, all humans, despite their many differences, will be equidistant from perfection, i.e., God.

The *A-mee-da* (Standing) Prayer

CONGREGANTS: PLEASE RISE.

Psalm 51:15

אֲדֹנָי, שְׂפָתַי תִּפְתָּח, וּפִי יַגִּיד תְּהִלָּתֶךָ:

A-do-nai, s'-fa-tai ti-f'-takh, u-fee ya-geed t'-hi-la-te-kha.

God, open my lips, and my mouth will declare Your glory.

Ancestors

בָּרוּךְ אַתָּה, יְיָ אֱלֹהֵינוּ וֵאלֹהֵי אֲבוֹתֵינוּ וְאִמּוֹתֵינוּ,

אֱלֹהֵי אַבְרָהָם,	אֱלֹהֵי שָׂרָה,
אֱלֹהֵי יִצְחָק,	אֱלֹהֵי רִבְקָה,
אֱלֹהֵי יַעֲקֹב,	אֱלֹהֵי רָחֵל וֵאלֹהֵי לֵאָה.

Ba-rukh A-ta, A-do-nai E-lo-hay-nu vAy-lo-hay a-vo-tay-nu v'-i-mo-tay-nu,

E-lo-hay A-v'-ra-ham,	*E-lo-hay Sa-ra,*
E-lo-hay Yi-ts'-khak,	*E-lo-hay Ri-v'-ka,*
E-lo-hay Ya-a-kov,	*E-lo-hay Ra-khayl vAy-lo-hay Lay-a.*

Bless You, [Eternal One]\[Who was, is, and will be], our God and God of our forefathers and foremothers,

God of Abraham,	**God of Sarah,**
God of Isaac,	**God of Rebecca,**
God of Jacob,	**God of Rachel and God of Leah.**

Exalted God,	*Ayl e-l'-yon,*	אֵל עֶלְיוֹן,
Bestower of benevolent favors.	*Go-mayl kha-sa-deem to-veem.*	גּוֹמֵל חֲסָדִים טוֹבִים.

The *A-mee*-da (Standing) Prayer Cont.

Sabbath

וְשָׁמְרוּ בְנֵי־יִשְׂרָאֵל אֶת־הַשַּׁבָּת, לַעֲשׂוֹת אֶת־הַשַּׁבָּת לְדֹרֹתָם בְּרִית עוֹלָם:

V'-sha-m'-ru v'-nay Yi-s'-ra-ayl et ha-Sha-bat, la-a-sot et ha-Sha-bat l'-do-ro-tam b'-reet o'-lam.

And the descendants of Israel will observe the Sabbath, participating in the Sabbath generation after generation as an everlasting covenant.

Exodus 31:16

אֱלֹהֵינוּ וֵאלֹהֵי אֲבוֹתֵינוּ: רְצֵה בִמְנוּחָתֵנוּ.

*E-lo-**hay**-nu vAy-lo-hay a-vo-**tay**-nu, r'-tsay vi-m'-nu-**kha**-**tay**-nu.*

Our God and God of our ancestors, be pleased with our rest.

Grant Peace

שִׂים שָׁלוֹם, טוֹבָה וּבְרָכָה, חֵן וָחֶסֶד וְרַחֲמִים, עָלֵינוּ, וְעַל־כָּל־יִשְׂרָאֵל {וְעַל כָּל גּוֹיֵי־הָאָרֶץ}.

*Seem sha-lom, to-va u-v'-ra-**kha**, **khayn** va-**khe**-sed v'-ra-**kha**-meem, a-**lay**-nu v'-al kawl Yi-s'-ra-ayl {v-al kawl go-yay ha-**a**-rets.}*

Grant peace, well-being, and blessing, grace and lovingkindness and mercy, to us, and to all Israel {and to all the nations of the earth.}

The *A-mee-da* (Standing) Prayer Cont.

Above are selected parts of the traditional *A-mee-da* (or Silent or Standing) Prayer, the central portion of the traditional prayer service. It ordinarily contains nineteen benedictions (statements starting בָּרוּךְ אַתָּה יְיָ **Bless You, [Eternal One]\[Who was, is, and will be]**), but on Sabbaths only seven grateful or celebratory benedictions are recited. Traditionally, the first recalls God's support for our patriarchs and matriarchs, and foretells that a redeemer will come; the second states that God supports the living, resurrects the dead, supports those who fall, heals the sick, and sets prisoners free; the third celebrates God's holiness. The fourth honors the Sabbath and recalls its faithful observance by Jews. The fifth asks God to accept our prayers and requests restoration of the Temple service; the sixth thanks God for God's moment-to-moment beneficence; the seventh requests God's ongoing gift of peace. In this book, the introductory portion is based on the version in קל הנשמה [*Kol ha-n'-sha-ma* **Voice of the Spirit**] 2nd Ed., The Reconstructionist Press, Elkins Park, PA: 2002, © 1996, The Reconstructionist Press.

Traditionally, the communal portions of this prayer are spoken softly so as not to disturb other worshipers' concentration, but loudly enough to be audible to the person praying, who should stand with feet together facing the Temple Mount in Jerusalem. Customarily, while praying, the worshiper pictures herself or himself standing before God-the-Sovereign. In keeping with this image, before starting this prayer, the worshiper takes three tiny steps forward, and at the end three backward, bowing leftward, then rightward, then forward, imitating the ancient way one approached and departed from a ruler. This may be puzzling, for God is everywhere. Surely we are not in God's presence only if we face in a specific direction and only if we step three steps forward. Therefore, this custom would appear intended to focus a worshiper's attention and induce a devotional mindset. However, it may have an undesirable side-effect. Maimonides (Rabbi Moses ben Maimon, 1135-1204) taught that in ancient times people originally understood that idols were not deities; people used idols as objects on which to focus attention during prayer. Over many generations, Maimonides believed, people gradually forgot that idols were not gods. We should beware of similar forgetfulness. God is not confined to the Temple Mount, nor is God present only when we pray.

Those who regularly recite the *A-mee-da* soon memorize it, despite its length. Many observant worshipers recite it very rapidly, but should continue to mean what they say. As Rabbi Aryeh Kaplan noted, the *A-mee-da*'s words comprise a long meditation mantra.

Following the communal *A-mee-da*, private meditation is customary.

Meditation

Below are readings that may facilitate meditation. Only a few are read in any one session. It is customary to remain standing while meditating. However, standing is not essential. One should meditate in the posture most conducive to meditation.

Psalm 92

According to tradition, this psalm was sung in the Temple by the Levites on Saturday. Consequently, it is customary to incorporate this psalm in "Welcoming the Sabbath" at the start of the Friday evening service. Since this psalm does not mention the Sabbath, some have questioned why it is sung then. Rabbi David Kimchi (1160-1235) stated that the psalm touches on profound issues whose consideration on weekdays may demand more time and energy than is available.

א מִזְמוֹר שִׁיר לְיוֹם הַשַּׁבָּת:

ב טוֹב לְהֹדוֹת לַייָ. > וּלְזַמֵּר לְשִׁמְךָ עֶלְיוֹן:

ג לְהַגִּיד בַּבֹּקֶר חַסְדֶּךָ. > וֶאֱמוּנָתְךָ בַּלֵּילוֹת:

ד עֲלֵי־עָשׂוֹר וַעֲלֵי־נָבֶל. > עֲלֵי הִגָּיוֹן בְּכִנּוֹר:

ה כִּי שִׂמַּחְתַּנִי יְיָ בְּפָעֳלֶךָ. > בְּמַעֲשֵׂי יָדֶיךָ אֲרַנֵּן:

ו מַה־גָּדְלוּ מַעֲשֶׂיךָ יְיָ. > מְאֹד עָמְקוּ מַחְשְׁבֹתֶיךָ:

ז אִישׁ־בַּעַר לֹא יֵדָע. > וּכְסִיל לֹא־יָבִין אֶת־זֹאת:

ח בִּפְרֹחַ רְשָׁעִים כְּמוֹ־עֵשֶׂב. > וַיָּצִיצוּ כָּל־פֹּעֲלֵי אָוֶן. > לְהִשָּׁמְדָם עֲדֵי־עַד:

ט וְאַתָּה מָרוֹם לְעֹלָם יְיָ:

י כִּי הִנֵּה אֹיְבֶיךָ יְיָ. > כִּי־הִנֵּה אֹיְבֶיךָ יֹאבֵדוּ. > יִתְפָּרְדוּ כָּל־פֹּעֲלֵי אָוֶן:

יא וַתָּרֶם כִּרְאֵים קַרְנִי. > בַּלֹּתִי בְּשֶׁמֶן רַעֲנָן:

יב וַתַּבֵּט עֵינִי בְּשׁוּרָי. > בַּקָּמִים עָלַי מְרֵעִים תִּשְׁמַעְנָה אָזְנָי:

יג צַדִּיק כַּתָּמָר יִפְרָח. > כְּאֶרֶז בַּלְּבָנוֹן יִשְׂגֶּה:

יד שְׁתוּלִים בְּבֵית יְיָ. > בְּחַצְרוֹת אֱלֹהֵינוּ יַפְרִיחוּ:

טו עוֹד יְנוּבוּן בְּשֵׂיבָה. > דְּשֵׁנִים וְרַעֲנַנִּים יִהְיוּ:

טז לְהַגִּיד כִּי־יָשָׁר יְיָ. > צוּרִי וְלֹא־עַוְלָתָה בּוֹ:

commons.wikimedia.org/wiki/File:Jerusalem_Model1_BW_2.JPG
by Berthold Werner/ Public Domain

Psalm 92 Cont.

1. <u>*Mi-z'-mor Sheer l'-Yom ha-Sha-bat*</u>

2. *Tov l'-ho-dot lA-do-nai, < > u-l'-za-mayr l'-shi-m'-<u>kha</u> e-l'-yon.*
3. *L'-ha-geed ba-**bo**-ker <u>kha</u>-s'-**de**-<u>kha</u>, < > ve-e-mu-na-t'-<u>kha</u> ba-lay-lot.*
4. *A-lay a-sor va-a-lay **na**-vel, < > a-lay hi-gai-on b'-<u>khi</u>-nor.*
5. *Kee si-ma-<u>kh</u>'-**ta**-nee A-do-nai b'-fa-a-**le**-<u>kha</u>, < > b'-ma-a-say ya-**day**-<u>kha</u> a-ra-nayn.*
6. *Ma ga-d'-lu ma-a-**say**-<u>kha</u> A-do-nai, < > m'-od a-m'-ku ma-<u>kh</u>'-sh'-vo-**tay**-<u>kha</u>.*
7. *Eesh **ba**-ar lo yay-da, < > u-<u>kh</u>'-seel lo ya-veen et zot:*
8. *bi-f'-**ro**-a<u>kh</u> r'-sha-eem k'-mo **ay**-sev, < > va-ya-**tsee**-tsu kawl po-a-lay **a**-ven, < > l'-hi-sha-m'-dam a-day ad,*
9. *v'-A-ta ma-rom l'-o-lam, A-do-nai,*
10. *kee hi-nay o-y'-**vay**-<u>kha</u>, A-do-nai, < > kee hi-nay o-y'-**vay**-<u>kha</u> yo-**vay**-du, < > yi-t'-pa-r'-du kawl **po**-a-lay **a**-ven*
11. *va-ta-rem ki-r'-aym ka-r'-nee. < > ba-lo-tee b'-**she**-men ra-a-nan,*
12. *va-ta-bayt ay-nee b'-shu-rai; < > ba-ka-meem a-lai m'-ray-eem, ti-sh'-**ma**-'-na a-z'-nai.*
13. *Tsa-deek ka-ta-mar yi-f'-ra<u>kh</u>, < > k'-**e**-rez ba-l'-va-non yi-s'-ge.*
14. *Sh'-tu-leem b'-vayt A-do-nai, < > b'-<u>kha</u>-ts'-rot E-lo-**hay**-nu ya-f'-**ree**-<u>khu</u>.*
15. *Od y'-nu-vun b'-say-va; < > d'-shay-neem v'-ra-a-na-neem yi-h'-yu,*
16. *l'-ha-geed kee ya-shar A-do-nai, < > Tsu-ree v'-lo a-v'-la-ta bo.*

1. **<u>A Song, A Poem for the Sabbath Day</u>**

2. **It is good to thank God < > and to sing to Your high name,**
3. **to tell in the morning about Your benevolence < > and Your faith\loyalty in the nights**
4. **on ten and on a stringed instrument, < > on the sound of a harp.**
5. **Because You have made me joyful, Lord, with Your deeds, < > of the work of Your hands I will sing.**
6. **How great Your works are, God! < > Your thoughts are very profound.**
7. **An ignorant person does not grasp < > and a fool would not understand this:**
8. **that the wicked flower like grass < > and that all doers of iniquity blossom < > is for their eternal destruction,**
9. **and You are forever highest, God,**
10. **because behold Your enemies, God, < > because behold Your enemies will perish, < > all doers of iniquity will be scattered**
11. **and You raise up my horn like wild oxen. < > I am anointed with fresh oil,**
12. **and You cause my eyes to behold my adversaries; < > when the wicked stand against me, You cause my ears to hear.**
13. **The righteous will blossom like a date palm, < > will flourish like a cedar of Lebanon.**
14. **Planted in God's house, < > they will flourish in the courtyards of our God.**
15. **In old age they will still be fruitful; < > they will be profuse and vigorous**
16. **to tell that God is honest, < > my Fortress, and in Whom is no injustice\unrighteousness\wrong.**

Psalm 92 Cont.

<u>A Song, a Poem for the Sabbath</u>

It does us good to feel grateful to God and to sing of Your high renown for benevolence;
whether morning or night,
whether communally or individually,
whether we deduce or intuit, we should be grateful.

For You have made me happy, God, by Your actions;
I will carol about Your personal deeds.
How great are Your works, God!
Your thoughts are very deep.
An ignorant person does not know, and a fool does not grasp this:
The sprouting of the wicked like grass and the blossoming of all evildoers is for their
  eternal destruction.
And You are high forever, my God.
For behold Your enemies, God, for behold, Your enemies shall be destroyed!
All evildoers shall be scattered.

And you fill me with vigor like wild oxen.
I am cared for and pampered.
You let me see what my enemies are up to, and hear their plans.

The righteous will blossom like a date palm,
will burgeon like a cedar of Lebanon.
Planted in God's estate, they will flourish in God's courtyards.
In old age, they will still be fruitful;
they will be productive and vigorous
and live to testify that God is righteous,
my refuge, in Whom there is no injustice.

Psalm 92 Cont.

The literal translation of the start of the fourth verse above is **On ten and on a stringed instrument.** Traditionally, it is translated as "On a ten-stringed harp." However, the Hebrew word נֶבֶל shares its three-letter root with a word that means **scoundrel**. Since, traditionally, a minimum of ten worshippers, a minyan, is required for a prayer service, an alternative non-traditional interpretation might be, "By a minyan and by a scoundrel [i.e., one who does not participate in prayer services]." The literal translation given above for the second half of that fourth verse is traditional. Hebrew words with related roots suggest a non-traditional translation: "On the basis of logic and on the basis of what seems to be so." Above, the translation of the twelfth verse is traditional. However, the Hebrew is somewhat obscure. Traditional authorities have offered various versions.

Starting with the seventh verse, the psalm addresses a (perhaps *the*) problem for those who believe in a good God: how can an omnipotent good God tolerate injustice, that sometimes the wicked prosper and the good or innocent suffer? This question is addressed in the Book of Job, where God's reply to Job may be interpreted to imply that the answer transcends Job's (or any human's) ability to comprehend.

There have been many other answers. Philosophers Epicurus and David Hume argued that God is either not omnipotent or not good. Some gnostics maintained that the Creator is not good. Other philosophers, e.g., Plato, John Stuart Mill, and Thomas Henry Huxley, suggested that God is not omnipotent. With this, writer H. G. Wells concurred. John Stuart Mill added that justice is probably not important to God. Philosopher William James concluded God is either not omnipotent or not omniscient. Philosopher Arthur Schopenhauer concluded that the universe is so flawed that God could not have created it. The psalmist asserts that prosperity by the wicked is, at most, a temporary aberration. Rashi suggested that the psalmist referred to the post-Messianic era, the "Great Sabbath," when there will be no injustice. According to Hindus and Hasidism's founder, Rabbi Israel ben Eliezer (1698-1760), the Good Master of the Name, justice is achieved by reincarnation; many Christians believe it is achieved by afterlife in heaven or hell; many Buddhists believe suffering, just or unjust, is transcended by detaching from life's lures and distractions. Catholic theologian, Thomas Aquinas, argued that injustice makes possible good aspects of God's creation otherwise impossible: For example, when the good or innocent suffer, they may exhibit the virtue of faithfully and trustingly enduring their misfortune. Philosopher Liebnitz argued that a world without evil is impossible, we live in the best possible world. Philosopher-historian Voltaire mocked this argument in his novella, *Candide*.

Kabbalists, such as Rabbi Isaac Ben Solomon Luria (1534-1572), believe that during creation God's infinite energy explosively intermingled good and evil; our task is to separate the good. Similar to this view, some Jewish mystics hold that injustice reflects flaws or "bugs" in God's creation that we humans were created to remedy [*tikkun*]. John Stuart Mill suggested that a limited God might need human help. Philosopher F. H. Bradley commented, if God's powers are limited, ultimately evil may win. If we humans help a limited God Whom evil defeats, we may become tragic heroes; we cannot count on good's triumph ensuring universal justice. Bradley added that if human logic concludes that injustice is incompatible with God's omnipotence, this may show that human logic does not apply to God. In the novel, *The Plague*, by Albert Camus, the atheist character, Dr. Bernard Rieux, strives to foster justice and alleviate suffering although he does not expect God's help.

Anything May Be Prayer If the Intent Is To Pray

Based on a Jewish folk tale

Once, the *Baal Shem Tov* [the Good Master of the Name] (Rabbi Israel ben Eliezer) was traveling in a carriage with some disciples. They passed a poorly dressed man jumping back and forth across a broad ditch next to the road. "Stop! Stop!" the *Baal Shem* called to the carriage driver. When the carriage had stopped, the *Baal Shem* leaped down onto the road and approached the man who was jumping back and forth.

"Why do you jump back and forth?" the *Baal Shem* asked.

The man replied: "I am poor and ignorant, but I want very much to honor God. I asked the wise men of my village how I could honor God, and they told me it would be very difficult for me to do so. That is all they would tell me. So I decided to do the most difficult thing I could think of. I remembered this ditch here beside the road. There is a saying in my village that this ditch is too wide for anyone to jump across. So every day for a year I practiced jumping until finally, today, I had grown able to jump across this ditch. Today, I am very happy, for at last I have found a way to honor God!"

The *Baal Shem Tov* turned to his disciples, who had gathered, and said. "This man's prayer is the most beautiful and most powerful that has been uttered anywhere today!"

This tale reflects the *Baal Shem*'s challenge to rabbinic elitism.

Eternal God, You overflow all human mind
defined infinities. Your timeless words began
Your universe of nested spheres with sparks entwined
in which we evanescent ones do what we can.

With faithful love for our return You yearn and wait
as, all about us, Your live glory burns in all.
But we have turned away to breed our sterile hate
as numbly toward "reality" we fall.

You know, not I, how long, as I, I'll live or will,
for only now and here are what my senses show
and trap me in their momentary pain or thrill.
How I am part of Your vast plan, You know.

    Now is now; I choose life; choice is just here.
    Soon brings death; use each breath; both trust and fear.

www.nasa.gov/mission_pages/spitzer/multimedia/spitzer-20070604.html /
NASA/JPL-Caltech/ESA/Harvard-Smithsonian CfA / Public Domain

Little Muttle's Prayer

Based on a Jewish folk tale

Muttle's family was the poorest in the shtetl. In those days, in that cruel land, education was much too expensive for poor folk like Dovid, his wife, Frumma, and their dear son, Muttle. When his parents could spare a few minutes from their never-ending labors, they tried to teach Muttle. By the time the boy was five, he had learned the Hebrew alphabet. Frumma and he would sing together, "*Alef, bays, gimmel, dalled...,*" while Frumma did her household chores.

On Muttle's sixth birthday, his parents promised him a special treat. Next Shabbos, for the first time, Muttle would accompany his father to shul for morning prayers! Muttle had often watched his father put on his tefillin, wrap himself in his tallis, and softly murmur his morning prayers at home. However, Muttle had never accompanied Dovid when he prayed with the minyan.

Muttle was beside himself with excitement. Being allowed to go to the minyan prayers meant to him that he was becoming a big boy. But he grew more and more worried. "What am I supposed to do?" he asked. "I don't know the prayers. I don't know how to read them in the siddur. Won't God be disappointed if I don't say the prayers like everyone else?"

"Don't worry, Muttle," his parents kept saying. God will understand that you are just a little boy. He will be pleased that you want to pray. Perhaps he will find a way for us to afford to send you to the cheder, so the rabbi will teach you how to read and pray.

Several times a day, Muttle asked his father, "What should I do while you and the rest of the men pray?" Over and over, Dovid answered, "Do what we do: stand when we stand; sit when we sit. Just don't fidget or chatter. Don't distract us while we are praying."

Dovid had started to feel a trifle impatient with his little son's repeated questions, so he was more glad than usual when Shabbos morning came. Dressed in their best albeit somewhat shabby clothes, father and son walked hand in hand to shul.

The two took a place in the last row, farthest from the Holy Ark, where humble Dovid usually sat. The little boy behaved well through most of the service: standing or sitting when the minyan did, never fidgeting or chattering. But Dovid had not mentioned that the morning service always concluded with *a capella* singing of *Adon Olam*. When the men began to sing, little Muttle also sang. However, instead of trying to sing the words of the hymn, he sang, "*Alef, bays, gimmel, dalled,...*" At the close of the first stanza, Dovid nudged his son and whispered, "*Shah!* [Hush!]" However, when the second stanza started, Muttle again sang "*Alef, bays,....*" Again, his father nudged him, whispering urgently, "*Shah,* Muttle, *Shah!*"

When the third stanza began, to Dovid's horror, the boy darted forward until he stood directly in front of the Ark. Above the men's voices, Muttle's treble could be heard saying, "I don't know how to read, but I do know that the letters of the alphabet make the words of every prayer. You know everything, God, and You can do anything! So, God, please take the letters I am giving You and put them together to make the prayer I should be singing!"

The minyan fell silent. The rabbi, an elderly Hasid, spoke up: "May our prayer be as sincere as the boy's!" Then, as the boy again sang "*Alef, bays, . . . ,*" everyone joined in.

Psalm 97

א יְיָ מָלָךְ, תָּגֵל הָאָרֶץ; יִשְׂמְחוּ אִיִּים רַבִּים.	1. A-do-nai ma-la*kh*, ta-**gayl** ha-**a**-rets; yi-s'-m'-*khu* ee-yeem ra-**beem**.
ב עָנָן וַעֲרָפֶל סְבִיבָיו; צֶדֶק וּמִשְׁפָּט מְכוֹן כִּסְאוֹ.	2. A-nan va-a-ra-fel s'-vee-vaiv; **tse**-dek u-mi-sh'-pat m'-*khon* ki-s'-o.
ג אֵשׁ, לְפָנָיו תֵּלֵךְ; וּתְלַהֵט סָבִיב צָרָיו.	3. Aysh, l'-fa-naiv tay-lay*kh*; u-t'-la-hayt sa-veev tsa-raiv.
ד הֵאִירוּ בְרָקָיו תֵּבֵל; רָאֲתָה וַתָּחֵל הָאָרֶץ.	4. Hay-ee-ru v'-ra-kaiv tay-vayl; ra-a-ta va-ta-*khayl* ha-**a**-rets.
ה הָרִים כַּדּוֹנַג, נָמַסּוּ מִלִּפְנֵי יְיָ: מִלִּפְנֵי, אֲדוֹן כָּל־הָאָרֶץ.	5. Ha-reem ka-do-nag, na-**ma**-su mi-li-f'-nay A-do-nai: mi-li-f'-nay, A-don kawl ha-**a**-rets.
ו הִגִּידוּ הַשָּׁמַיִם צִדְקוֹ; וְרָאוּ כָל־הָעַמִּים כְּבוֹדוֹ.	6. Hi-**gee**-du ha-sha-**ma**-yim tsi-d'-ko; v'-ra-u *khawl* ha-a-meem k'-vo-do.
ז יֵבֹשׁוּ, כָּל־עֹבְדֵי פֶסֶל הַמִּתְהַלְלִים בָּאֱלִילִים; הִשְׁתַּחֲווּ־לוֹ, כָּל־אֱלֹהִים.	7. Yay-**vo**-shu, kawl o-v'-day **pe**-sel ha-mi-t'-ha-l'-leem ba-e-lee-leem; hi-sh'-ta-*kha*-vu lo, kawl e-lo-heem.
ח שָׁמְעָה וַתִּשְׂמַח, צִיּוֹן, וַתָּגֵלְנָה, בְּנוֹת יְהוּדָה לְמַעַן מִשְׁפָּטֶיךָ יְיָ.	8. Sha-m'-a va-ti-s'-ma*kh*, Tsee-yon, va-ta-**gay**-l'-na, b'-not Y'-hu-da l'-**ma**- an mi-sh'-pa-**tay**-*kha* A-do-nai.
ט כִּי־אַתָּה יְיָ, עֶלְיוֹן עַל־כָּל־הָאָרֶץ; מְאֹד נַעֲלֵיתָ, עַל־כָּל־אֱלֹהִים.	9. Kee a-ta A-do-nai, e-l'-yon al kawl ha-**a**-rets; m'-od na-a-**lay**-ta, al kawl e-lo-heem.
י אֹהֲבֵי יְיָ, שִׂנְאוּ רָע: שֹׁמֵר, נַפְשׁוֹת חֲסִידָיו; מִיַּד רְשָׁעִים, יַצִּילֵם.	10. O-ha-vay A-do-nai, si-n'-u ra: sho-mayr, na-f'-shot *kha*-see-daiv; mi-yad r'-sha-eem, ya-tsee-laym.
יא אוֹר, זָרֻעַ לַצַּדִּיק; וּלְיִשְׁרֵי־לֵב שִׂמְחָה.	11. Or, za-**ru**-a la-tsa-deek; u-l'-yi-sh'-ray layv si-m'-*kha*.
יב שִׂמְחוּ צַדִּיקִים, בַּיְיָ; וְהוֹדוּ, לְזֵכֶר קָדְשׁוֹ.	12. Si-m'-*khu* tsa-dee-keem, ba-A-do-nai; v'-ho-du, l'-**zay**-*kher* ka-d'-sho.

Psalm 97 Cont.

1. When God's sovereignty will have come about, the earth will rejoice, the many islands will be glad!

2. Surrounded by clouds and darkness, righteousness and justice are the foundation of God's throne.

3. Fire precedes God, and burns up God's encompassing enemies.

4. God's lightnings lit up the world; the earth saw and trembled.

5. The mountains melted before God like wax, before the Ruler of the whole world.

6. The heavens declared God's righteousness, and the nations saw God's glory.

7. All who serve statues, who pray to idols, should be ashamed; bow to God, all you godlets!

8. Zion heard and was glad, and the daughters of Judah rejoiced because of Your judgments, God.

9. For You, God, are high above all the earth; You are exalted far above all godlets.

10. Hate evil, you lovers of God, Who protects the souls of God's pious ones from the grip of the wicked.

11. Light is sown for the righteous, and joy for those with upright hearts.

12. Be glad about God, you righteous ones, and give thanks for the memory of God's holiness.

Psalm 121

א שִׁיר, לַמַּעֲלוֹת:
אֶשָּׂא עֵינַי אֶל־הֶהָרִים מֵאַיִן יָבֹא עֶזְרִי.
ב עֶזְרִי מֵעִם יְיָ עֹשֵׂה שָׁמַיִם וָאָרֶץ
ג אַל־יִתֵּן לַמּוֹט רַגְלֶךָ אַל־יָנוּם שֹׁמְרֶךָ.
ד הִנֵּה לֹא־יָנוּם וְלֹא יִישָׁן שׁוֹמֵר יִשְׂרָאֵל.
ה יְיָ שֹׁמְרֶךָ יְיָ צִלְּךָ עַל־יַד יְמִינֶךָ.
ו יוֹמָם הַשֶּׁמֶשׁ לֹא־יַכֶּכָּה וְיָרֵחַ בַּלָּיְלָה.
ז יְיָ יִשְׁמָרְךָ מִכָּל־רָע יִשְׁמֹר אֶת־נַפְשֶׁךָ.
ח יְיָ יִשְׁמָר־צֵאתְךָ וּבוֹאֶךָ מֵעַתָּה וְעַד־עוֹלָם.

Death Valley salt desert mountains (http://www.-public-domain-image.com/full-image/nature-landscapes-public-domain-images-pictures/valley-public-domain-images-pictures/death-valley-salt-desert-mountains.jpg-free-stock-photo.html) by Jon Sullivan/ Public Domain

Psalm 121 Cont.

1. *Sheer, la-ma-a-lot:*
   *E-sa ay-nai el he-ha-reem may-**a**-yin ya-vo e-z'-ree.*
2. *E-z'-ree may-im A-do-nai o-say sha-ma-yim va-**a**-rets*
3. *Al yi-tayn la-mot ra-g'-**le**-kha al ya-num Sho-m'-**re**-kha.*
4. *Hi-nay lo ya-num v'-lo yee-shan Sho-mayr Yi-s'-ra-ayl.*
5. *A-do-nai sho-m'-**re**-kha A-do-nai tsi-l'-kha al yad y'-mee-**ne**-kha.*
6. *Yo-mam ha-**she**-mesh lo ya-**ke**-ka v'-ya-**ray**-akh ba-**lai**-y'-la.*
7. *A-do-nai yi-sh'-ma-r'-kha mi-kawl ra yi-sh'-mor et na-f'-**she**-kha.*
8. *A-do-nai yi-sh'-mar tsay-t'-kha u-vo-e-kha may-a-ta v'-ad o-lam.*

1. **A song\poem about degrees\ascents:**
   When I raise my eyes toward the mountains [where will help come from for me?]\[help will come for me from the void*].
2. **My help is from the Eternal maker of heavens and earth.**
3. **Your Protector will neither slumber nor allow your foot to slip.**
4. **Behold! Israel's Protector will neither slumber nor sleep.**
5. **The Eternal protects you; the Eternal [beside you shades]\[is your shadow next to] your right hand.**
6. **By day the sun will not harm you, nor the moon at night.**
7. **The Eternal will guard you from all harm\evil, will protect your soul.**
8. **The Eternal will guard your going and your coming from now until forever.**

---

*The second alternative translation derives from a suggestion by Sylvia Boorstein, a Buddhist observant Jew.

The Eight Degrees of Charity

There are eight degrees in the giving of charity, each successively higher:

- One who gives grudgingly.

- One who gives cheerfully, but not enough.

- One who gives a sufficient sum, but only when asked.

- One who gives before being asked, and directly to the needy.

- One who gives so that the needy knows the identity of the source, but the giver does not know the identity of the recipient.

- One who gives so that the giver knows the identity of the recipient, but the recipient does not know the identity of the giver.

- One who gives so that the giver does not know the identity of the recipient, nor does the recipient know the identity of the giver.

- The highest form: One who helps the needy by offering a gift or a loan, or by joining in a partnership, or by providing work, so that the person may become self-supporting.

Based on commentary by Maimonides

Rabbi Moses ben Maimon
commons.wikimedia.org/wiki/File:Maimonides-2.jpg
by Blaisio Ugolino/ Public Domain

Psalm 19:1-10

א לַמְנַצֵּחַ מִזְמוֹר לְדָוִד׃

ב הַשָּׁמַיִם מְסַפְּרִים כְּבוֹד־אֵל
וּמַעֲשֵׂה יָדָיו מַגִּיד הָרָקִיעַ׃

ג יוֹם לְיוֹם יַבִּיעַ אֹמֶר
וְלַיְלָה לְּלַיְלָה יְחַוֶּה־דָּעַת׃

ד אֵין־אֹמֶר וְאֵין דְּבָרִים
בְּלִי נִשְׁמָע קוֹלָם׃

ה בְּכָל־הָאָרֶץ יָצָא קַוָּם
וּבִקְצֵה תֵבֵל מִלֵּיהֶם
לַשֶּׁמֶשׁ שָׂם אֹהֶל בָּהֶם׃

ו וְהוּא כְּחָתָן יֹצֵא מֵחֻפָּתוֹ
יָשִׂישׂ כְּגִבּוֹר לָרוּץ אֹרַח׃

ז מִקְצֵה הַשָּׁמַיִם מוֹצָאוֹ
וּתְקוּפָתוֹ עַל־קְצוֹתָם
וְאֵין נִסְתָּר מֵחַמָּתוֹ׃

ח תּוֹרַת יְיָ תְּמִימָה מְשִׁיבַת נָפֶשׁ
עֵדוּת יְיָ נֶאֱמָנָה מַחְכִּימַת פֶּתִי׃

ט פִּקּוּדֵי יְיָ יְשָׁרִים מְשַׂמְּחֵי־לֵב
מִצְוַת יְיָ בָּרָה מְאִירַת עֵינָיִם׃

י יִרְאַת יְיָ טְהוֹרָה עוֹמֶדֶת לָעַד
מִשְׁפְּטֵי־יְיָ אֱמֶת צָדְקוּ יַחְדָּו׃

Psalm 19:1-10 Cont.

1. *La-m'-na-tsay-a<u>kh</u> Mi-z'-mor l'-Da-vid:*

2. *Ha-sha-**ma**-yim m'-sa-p'-reem k'-vod Ayl*
*u-ma-a-say ya-daiv ma-geed ha-ra-**kee**-ya.*

    3. *Yom l'-yom ya-**bee**-ya o-mer*
*v'-**la**-y'-la l'-**la**-y'-la y'-<u>kh</u>a-ve **da**-at.*

    4. *Ayn **o**-mer v'-ayn d'-va-reem*
b'-lee ni-sh'-ma ko-lam.

    5. *B'-<u>kh</u>awl ha-**a**-rets ya-tsa ka-vam*
u-vi-k'-tsay tay-vayl mi-lay-hem
*la-**she**-mesh sam **o**-hel ba-hem.*

    6. *V'-hu k'-<u>kh</u>a-tan yo-tsay may-<u>kh</u>u-pa-to*
*ya-sees k'-gi-bor la-ruts **o**-ra<u>kh</u>.*

    7. *Mi-k'-tsay ha-sha-**ma**-yim mo-tsa-o*
u-t'-ku-fa-to al k'-tso-tam
v'-ayn ni-s'-tar may-<u>kh</u>a-ma-to.

8. *To-rat A-do-nai t'-mee-ma m'-**shee**-vat **na**-fesh*
*ay-dut A-do-nai ne-e-ma-na ma-<u>kh</u>'-**kee**-mat **pe**-tee.*

9. *Pi-ku-day A-do-nai y'-sha-reem m'-sa-m'-<u>kh</u>ay layv*
*mi-ts'-vat A-do-nai ba-ra m'-ee-rat ay-**na**-yim.*

10. *Yi-r'-at A-do-nai t'-ho-ra o-**me**-det la-ad*
mi-sh'-p'-tay A-do-nai e-met tsa-d'-ku ya-<u>kh</u>'-dav.

Psalm 19:1-10 Cont.

1. For the conductor: A psalm by David

2. The heavens proclaim God's glory
And the celestial sphere preaches about God's handiwork.

3. Day to day speaks
And night to night makes known knowledge.

4. There is no speech and there are no words
Without their voices being heard.

5. Their communications stretch across the whole world,
And their words to the ends of the earth.
God has set a tent there for the sun,

6. Which is radiant like a bridegroom coming out of his wedding chamber,
Rejoicing like an athlete experiencing runner's high.

7. Its origin is at the far ends of the heavens
And its period extends across them;
Nothing is hidden from its heat.

8. God's Torah is perfect, restoring the soul;
God's testimony is trustworthy, making the unsophisticated wise;

9. God's precepts are just, delighting the heart;
God's commandment is lucid, illuminating the eyes.

10. Awe of God is pure, enduring forever;
God's verdicts are true, altogether just.

Sunset by rock (www.public-domain-image.com/nature-landscapes-public-domain-images-pictures/sunset-public-domain-images-pictures/sunset-by-rock.jpg.html)/ Public Domain

Ts'daka [Charity] in Our Lives

Our sages taught: The giving of *ts'daka* is as great as all the other mitzvoth together. – Bava Batra 9a

In *ts'daka* there are two hands: One that gives and one that receives. Be grateful that yours is a hand that can give. – Midrash Tanhuma

Let us give *ts'daka* generously, for we are as big as our capacity to share.

We make a living by what we get; we make a life by what we give.

Each day we receive blessings without number. May each day, therefore, find us sharing our blessings. – Siddur *Hadash*

As we feed, we are fed.
As we give, we receive. – Rabbi Yosil Rosenzweig

As we lift, we are raised. – Glen I. Hitchcock

So let us share our God-given blessings gratefully and generously, regularly and joyously!

commons.wikimedia.org/wiki/File:PikiWiki_Israel_14886_Blue_box.JPG
©ארכיון הצילומים קקל, פנינה לבני / Wikimedia Commons / CC-BY-2.5
(http://creativecommons.org/license/by/2.5/)
Creative Commons Attribution 2.5 Generic license

Judaism's Tradition of Commentary and Debate

Our tradition includes many generations of lively commentary and debate. For instance, the Cairo genizah [collection of discarded texts] contains references to questions by a ninth-century skeptic, Hiwi al-Balkhi, who asked, e.g., Why did God make humans vulnerable to suffering? Why does the Bible contain so many internal contradictions?

About such issues and many others, our sages have debated for more than two thousand years. For example, they continue to debate whether we are commanded by God to believe in God. Related is controversy about whether the first of the Ten Commandments is really a commandment. Some deny that it commands us to believe in God, arguing that if (*a*) a person already believed in God, God would have no reason to command the person to do so, while if (*b*) a person did not believe in God, God's command would be unlikely to have much influence. Therefore, God would not "waste" a commandment that was either unnecessary or unlikely to be obeyed.

Some have argued that belief in God requires a "leap of faith" that cannot be based solely on reason or logic. Consequently, particularly in recent times, the question, "Does God exist?" has come to be regarded by some as not subject to a conclusive answer.

Related questions, also much debated for many centuries, include: "Does believing in God do a person good?" and "Is it good for a group of people that they collectively believe in God?" Those who answer "Yes" sometimes argue that belief in God is necessary to prevent individuals or societies from descending to self-destructively selfish or self-indulgent lifestyles. This answer is related to the view that people are naturally or innately evil, itself debatable. Those who answer "No" may point to occasions when people did obviously unjust, immoral, unethical, or cruel acts, claiming that God commanded them to do so.

Some have suggested that belief in God evolved because it favored survival. For example, philosopher Daniel Dennett suggested that belief in God may act as a placebo: Believers, buoyed by their faith, may be more likely to recover from serious illness. One may also suspect that belief in a tribal God evolved because it led individuals to sacrifice themselves for the welfare of fellow members of their tribe. Note: whether belief in God evolved has no logical relevance to whether God exists.

Among related views that many of our sages generally agree about: Living a life in obedience to the 613 commandments is logically and practically distinct from believing in God. Everyday experience, they note, reveals that belief in God does not necessarily lead a person consistently to obey all the commandments. Moreover, most sages assert, it is wise to live in obedience to God's commandments, even if one doubts God's existence.

Prayer Is Not Enough: We Must Also Act

Based on a Jewish folk tale

There was once upon a time a pious but poor Jewish man who fervently wished that he were wealthy. At every prayer service, and many times between services, he would pray to God for wealth. He was a good man, and so he did not want the wealth for himself alone. Rather, he yearned to be able to give generous gifts to the poor. "Oh, God," he would whisper during the personal meditation portion of the Standing Prayer, "if only You would let me become wealthy, for example, let me win the lottery! I swear I would give all my riches to those deserving charity, and so through my good fortune You could give blessings to so many!" Years passed and the man began to grow elderly. Still, he never stopped praying for wealth and promising to use the wealth for good. For every day of his adult life he prayed the same prayer and promised the same promise at least five times. Finally, old and weak, he changed his prayer. "Why, God," he whispered, "have you not granted what I have begged for? In what way have I failed?"

A Voice came to him from somewhere high above: "Why have you never bought a lottery ticket?"

We must do more than merely pray for war to cease:
Each day our actions help make war – or peace.
When we encounter storm and rage in daily living,
Peace needs our patience, kindness, and forgiving.

We must do more than merely pray disease should end:
We each must help our injured neighbors mend.
Whether they suffer in body, mind, or soul,
They need our caring love to make them whole.

We must do more than merely pray to end injustice:
Show those who were wronged why they should trust us.
It does not matter whether we share the guilt,
Only by our efforts will a better world be built.

We must do more than merely pray to end despair:
God expects of us *tikkun:* our help repair
The universe, our help reveal the Light
That God created before day and night.

Maimonides proclaimed what he considered to be "The Thirteen Principles of Jewish Faith."

Each Principle starts with "I believe with perfect faith that . . . " and continues –

1. God is the Creator and Ruler of all things. Only God made, makes, and will make all things;
2. God is One. There is no unity in any way like God's. Only God is our God, Who was, is, and will be;
3. God does not have a body. Physical concepts do not apply to God. Nothing whatsoever resembles God in any way;
4. God is first and last;
5. only to God is it proper to pray; one may not pray to anyone or anything else;
6. all the statements of the prophets are true;
7. the prophecy of Moses is absolutely true; he was the chief of all prophets, both before and after him;
8. the entire Torah we now have is what was given to Moses;
9. the Torah will not be changed, and God will never give another one;
10. God knows all human deeds and thoughts. It is thus written (Psalm 33:15), "God has molded every heart together; God understands what each one does";
11. God rewards those who keep God's commandments, and punishes those who transgress them;
12. the Messiah will come; no matter how long it takes, I will await the Messiah's coming every day;
13. the dead will be brought back to life when God wills it to happen.

Like so much else in Jewish tradition, the Thirteen Principles have been controversial. The last Principle has been questioned by many authorities. The Spanish philosopher, Rabbi Joseph Albo (1380-1444), disputed the 12th Principle. Franz Kafka, among others, suggested that the Messiah will come only when he is no longer necessary. Perhaps, while we await the coming of one individual in whose person will be concentrated all messianic attributes, we collectively comprise a distributed Messiah who manifests whenever one of us acts as the Messiah would act. If this is so, then we are collectively responsible not only to await the Messiah but also to be the Messiah. Elie Wiesel expressed a similar thought.

On p. 64 below, the hymn, *Yi-g'-dal*, roughly parallels the Thirteen Principles.

Isaiah 1:11-17

יא "לָמָּה־לִּי רֹב־זִבְחֵיכֶם" יֹאמַר יְיָ, "שָׂבַעְתִּי עֹלוֹת אֵילִים וְחֵלֶב מְרִיאִים;
וְדַם פָּרִים וּכְבָשִׂים וְעַתּוּדִים, לֹא חָפָצְתִּי:

יב "כִּי תָבֹאוּ, לֵרָאוֹת פָּנָי – מִי־בִקֵּשׁ זֹאת מִיֶּדְכֶם, רְמֹס חֲצֵרָי:

יג "לֹא תוֹסִיפוּ, הָבִיא מִנְחַת־שָׁוְא – קְטֹרֶת תּוֹעֵבָה הִיא לִי; חֹדֶשׁ וְשַׁבָּת
קְרֹא מִקְרָא, לֹא־אוּכַל אָוֶן וַעֲצָרָה:

יד "חָדְשֵׁיכֶם וּמוֹעֲדֵיכֶם שָׂנְאָה נַפְשִׁי הָיוּ עָלַי לָטֹרַח; נִלְאֵיתִי, נְשֹׂא:

טו "וּבְפָרִשְׂכֶם כַּפֵּיכֶם, אַעְלִים עֵינַי מִכֶּם – גַּם כִּי־תַרְבּוּ תְפִלָּה, אֵינֶנִּי שֹׁמֵעַ;
יְדֵיכֶם, דָּמִים מָלֵאוּ:

טז "רַחֲצוּ, הִזַּכּוּ – הָסִירוּ רֹעַ מַעַלְלֵיכֶם מִנֶּגֶד עֵינָי; חִדְלוּ, הָרֵעַ:

יז "לִמְדוּ הֵיטֵב, דִּרְשׁוּ מִשְׁפָּט, אַשְּׁרוּ חָמוֹץ; שִׁפְטוּ יָתוֹם, רִיבוּ אַלְמָנָה."

11. "La-ma lee rov zi-v'-<u>kh</u>ay-<u>kh</u>em" yo-mar A-do-nai, "sa-va-'-tee o-lot ay-leem v'-<u>kh</u>ay-lev m'-ree-eem; v'-dam pa-reem u-<u>kh</u>'-va-seem v'-a-tu-deem, lo <u>kh</u>a-fa-ts'-tee.
12. "Kee ta-vo-u lay-ra-ot pa-nai -- mee vi-kaysh zot mi-ye-d'-<u>kh</u>em, r'-mos <u>kh</u>a-tsay-rai.
13. "Lo to-see-fu ha-vee mi-n'-<u>kh</u>at sha-v' -- k'-to-ret to-ay-va hee lee; <u>kh</u>o-desh v'-sha-bat k'ro mi-k'-ra, lo u-<u>kh</u>al a-ven va-a-tsa-ra.
14. "<u>Kh</u>a-d'-shay-<u>kh</u>em u-mo-a-day-<u>kh</u>em sa-n'-a na-f'-shee, ha-yu a-lai la-to-ra<u>kh</u>; ni-l'ay-tee, n'-so.
15. "U-v'-fa-ri-s'-<u>kh</u>em ka-pay-<u>kh</u>em, a-'-leem ay-nai mi-kem -- gam kee ta-r'-bu t'-fi-la, ay-ne-nee sho-may-a; y'-day-<u>kh</u>em, da-meem ma-**lay**-u.
16. "Ra-<u>kh</u>a-tsu, hi-za-ku -- ha-see-ru ro-a ma-a-l'-lay-<u>kh</u>em mi-ne-ged ay-nai; <u>kh</u>i-d'-lu, ha-ray-a.
17. "Li-m'-du hay-tayv, di-r'-shu mi-sh'-pat, a-sh'-ru <u>kh</u>a-mots; shi-f'-tu ya-tom, ree-vu a-l'-ma-na."

11. God says, "Why do you sacrifice so much to Me? I am satiated with your burnt offerings of rams and fat from oxen; and I do not appreciate the blood of bulls or lambs or he-goats.

12. "For, when you come to present yourselves before Me – who asked this of you, trampling My courts?

13. "Do not add more useless offerings – incense that is to Me an abomination; I do not relish new moon and sabbath [ceremonies], readings from the Bible, or [religious] convocations.

14. "I detest your new-moon and seasonal ceremonies; they are a burden to Me; I am tired of supporting them.

15. "And when you spread your hands, I will hide My eyes from you – also when you make many prayers, I will not listen: your hands are covered with blood.

16. "Wash yourselves, clean up – rid yourselves of the evil that is upon you, that is before My eyes; cease the wickedness.

17. "Learn to do good, seek justice, relieve the oppressed; deal fairly with an orphan, plead for a widow."

The prophet lists (*a*) various specific observances that God requires, (*b*) examples of more general just, moral behavior. God, he tells us, rejects our specific observances if we do not live justly and morally. See also the selection from Micah immediately below.

Micah 6:8

הִגִּיד לְךָ אָדָם, מַה־טּוֹב; וּמָה־יְיָ דּוֹרֵשׁ מִמְּךָ, כִּי אִם־עֲשׂוֹת מִשְׁפָּט וְאַהֲבַת חֶסֶד, וְהַצְנֵעַ לֶכֶת, עִם־אֱלֹהֶיךָ.

Hi-geed l'-*kha* a-dam, ma tov; u-ma A-do-nai do-raysh mi-m'-*kha*, kee im a-sot mi-sh'-pat v'-**a**-ha-vat *khe*-sed, v'-ha-ts'-**nay**-a le-*khet*, im E-lo-**hay**-*kha*.

You are informed, human, what is good; and what God demands of you is just to behave justly and love mercy, and walk modestly with your God.

Isaiah 42:1-7

א "הֵן עַבְדִּי אֶתְמָךְ־בּוֹ, בְּחִירִי רָצְתָה נַפְשִׁי; נָתַתִּי רוּחִי עָלָיו, מִשְׁפָּט לַגּוֹיִם יוֹצִיא.

1. "Hayn a-v'-dee e-t'-ma*kh* bo, b'-*khee*-ree ra-ts'-ta na-f'-shee; na-ta-tee ru-*khee* a-laiv, mi-sh'-pat la-go-yim yo-tsee.

ב "לֹא יִצְעַק, וְלֹא יִשָּׂא; וְלֹא־יַשְׁמִיעַ בַּחוּץ, קוֹלוֹ.

2. "Lo yi-ts'-ak, v'-lo yi-sa; v'lo ya-sh'-mee-a ba-*khuts*, ko-lo.

ג "קָנֶה רָצוּץ לֹא יִשְׁבּוֹר, וּפִשְׁתָּה כֵהָה לֹא יְכַבֶּנָּה; לֶאֱמֶת, יוֹצִיא מִשְׁפָּט.

3. "Ka-ne ra-tsuts lo yi-sh'-bor, u-fi-sh'-ta *khay*-ha lo y'-*kha*-be-na; le-e-met, yo-tsee mi-sh'-pat.

ד "לֹא יִכְהֶה וְלֹא יָרוּץ, עַד־יָשִׂים בָּאָרֶץ מִשְׁפָּט; וּלְתוֹרָתוֹ, אִיִּים יְיַחֵלוּ."

4. "Lo yi-*kh*'-he v'-lo ya-ruts, ad ya-seem ba-**a**-rets mi-sh'-pat; u-l-to-ra-to, ee-yeem y'-ya-*khay*-lu."

ה כֹּה־אָמַר הָאֵל יְיָ, בּוֹרֵא הַשָּׁמַיִם וְנוֹטֵיהֶם, רֹקַע הָאָרֶץ, וְצֶאֱצָאֶיהָ; נֹתֵן נְשָׁמָה לָעָם עָלֶיהָ, וְרוּחַ לַהֹלְכִים בָּהּ.

5. Ko a-mar ha-Ayl A-do-nai, Bo-ray ha-sha-ma-yim v'-no-tay-hem, ro-ka ha-**a**-rets, v'-tse-e-tsa-ay-a; no-tayn n'-sha-ma la-am a-lay-a, v'-ru-a*kh* la-ho-l'-*kheem* ba:

ו "אֲנִי יְיָ קְרָאתִיךָ בְצֶדֶק, וְאַחְזֵק בְּיָדֶךָ; וְאֶצָּרְךָ, וְאֶתֶּנְךָ לִבְרִית עָם – לְאוֹר גּוֹיִם.

6. "A-nee A-do-nai k'-ra-tee-*kha* v'-tse-dek, v'-a-*kh*'-zayk b'-ya-de-*kha*; v'-e-tsa-r'-*kha*, v'-e-te-n'-*kha* li-v'-reet am – l'-or go-yim.

ז "לִפְקֹחַ, עֵינַיִם עִוְרוֹת; לְהוֹצִיא מִמַּסְגֵּר אַסִּיר, מִבֵּית כֶּלֶא יֹשְׁבֵי חֹשֶׁךְ."

7. "Li-f'-ko-a*kh*, ay-na-yim i-v'-rot; l'-ho-tsee mi-ma-s'-gayr a-seer, mi-bayt ke-le yo-sh'-vay *kho*-she*kh*."

1 "To My servant, whom I support, My chosen one, who delights Me, surely I have given My spirit; he shall make laws go out to the nations.
2 "He shall not bellow, nor lift up, nor cause his voice to be heard outdoors.
3 "He shall not break a bruised reed, nor shall he quench a smoldering wick; he shall make laws go forth according to the truth.
4 "He shall neither become enfeebled nor be appeased till he have put laws in the earth, and the isles shall await his teaching."
5 This is what God the Eternal says, Who created the heavens and extended them, having spread out the earth and that which grows out of it, gives breath to the people upon it, and spirit to those who walk on it:
6 "I, the Eternal, have called you in righteousness, and have strengthened your hand and preserved you, and made you the people's covenant – a light for the nations,
7 "To open blind eyes, bring out prisoners locked in dungeons, and out of prisons those who sit in darkness."

Isaiah 42:1-7 Continued

The "servant" in the selection above is identified with the Messiah by some, the Jewish people by others. With either interpretation, the text exemplifies our traditions of abstaining from proselytizing and trying to be a role model for other peoples.

Isaiah 56:1-7

א כֹּה אָמַר יְיָ "שִׁמְרוּ מִשְׁפָּט וַעֲשׂוּ צְדָקָה כִּי־קְרוֹבָה יְשׁוּעָתִי לָבוֹא וְצִדְקָתִי לְהִגָּלוֹת"

ב אַשְׁרֵי אֱנוֹשׁ יַעֲשֶׂה־זֹּאת וּבֶן־אָדָם יַחֲזִיק בָּהּ שֹׁמֵר שַׁבָּת מֵחַלְּלוֹ וְשֹׁמֵר יָדוֹ מֵעֲשׂוֹת כָּל־רָע

ג וְאַל־יֹאמַר בֶּן־הַנֵּכָר הַנִּלְוָה אֶל־יְיָ לֵאמֹר "הַבְדֵּל יַבְדִּילַנִי יְיָ מֵעַל עַמּוֹ" וְאַל־יֹאמַר הַסָּרִיס "הֵן אֲנִי עֵץ יָבֵשׁ"

ד כִּי־כֹה אָמַר יְיָ לַסָּרִיסִים "אֲשֶׁר יִשְׁמְרוּ אֶת־שַׁבְּתוֹתַי וּבָחֲרוּ בַּאֲשֶׁר חָפָצְתִּי וּמַחֲזִיקִים בִּבְרִיתִי

ה "וְנָתַתִּי לָהֶם בְּבֵיתִי וּבְחוֹמֹתַי יָד וָשֵׁם טוֹב מִבָּנִים וּמִבָּנוֹת שֵׁם עוֹלָם אֶתֶּן־לוֹ אֲשֶׁר לֹא יִכָּרֵת

ו "וּבְנֵי הַנֵּכָר הַנִּלְוִים עַל־יְיָ לְשָׁרְתוֹ וּלְאַהֲבָה אֶת־שֵׁם יְיָ לִהְיוֹת לוֹ לַעֲבָדִים כָּל־שֹׁמֵר שַׁבָּת מֵחַלְּלוֹ וּמַחֲזִיקִים בִּבְרִיתִי

ז "וַהֲבִיאוֹתִים אֶל־הַר קָדְשִׁי וְשִׂמַּחְתִּים בְּבֵית תְּפִלָּתִי עוֹלֹתֵיהֶם וְזִבְחֵיהֶם לְרָצוֹן עַל־מִזְבְּחִי כִּי בֵיתִי בֵּית־תְּפִלָּתִי יִקָּרֵא לְכָל־הָעַמִּים"

1. Ko a-mar A-do-nai: "Shi-m'-ru mi-sh'-pat va-a-su ts'-da-ka kee k'-ro-va y'-shu-a-tee la-vo v'-tsi-d'-ka-tee l'-hi-ga-lot."
2. A-sh'-ray e-nosh ya-a-se zot u-ven a-dam ya-<u>kha</u>-zeek ba; sho-mayr sha-bat may-<u>kha</u>-l'-lo v'-sho-mayr ya-do may-a-sot kawl ra.
3. V'-al yo-mar ben ha-nay-<u>khar</u> ha-ni-l'-va el A-do-nai lay-mor: "Ha-v'-dayl ya-v'-dee-la-nee A-do-nai may-al a-mo" v'-al yo-mar ha-sa-rees "Hayn a-nee ayts ya-vaysh."
4. Kee <u>kho</u> a-mar A-do-nai la-sa-ree-seem "A-sher yi-sh'-m'-ru et sha-b'-to-tai u-va-<u>kha</u>-ru ba-a-sher <u>kha</u>-fa-ts'-tee u-ma-<u>kha</u>-zee-keem bi-v'-ree-tee
5. "v'-na-ta-tee la-hem b'-vay-tee u-v'-<u>kho</u>-mo-tai yad va-shaym; tov mi-ba-neem u-mi-ba-not shaym o-lam e-ten lo a-sher lo yi-ka-rayt
6. "u-v'-nay ha-nay-<u>khar</u> ha-ni-l'-veem al A-do-nai l'-sha-r'-to u-l'-a-ha-va et shaym A-do-nai li-h'-yot lo la-a-va-deem kawl sho-mayr sha-bat may-<u>kha</u>-l'-lo u-ma-<u>kha</u>-zee-keem bi-v'-ree-tee
7. "va-ha-vee-o-teem el har ka-d'-shee v'-si-ma-<u>kh</u>'-teem b'-vayt t'-fi-la-tee o-lo-tay-hem v'-zi-v'-<u>khay</u>-hem l'-ra-tson al mi-z'-b'-<u>khee</u>, kee vay-tee bayt t'-fi-la-tee yi-ka-ray l'-<u>khawl</u> ha-a-meem."

Isaiah 56:1-7 Cont.

1. **Here is what God says: "Obey just laws and be just\charitable, for My salvation is coming soon, and My justice\charity for the exiled."**
2. **The person who does this is happy, and so is the mortal who clings to it, who observes the Sabbath, not profaning it, and guards his hand from doing any wrong.**
3. **Nor should a non-Israelite\[cut-off person] who is connected with God say, "God will certainly separate me from God's people"; nor should a eunuch say, "Ah yes, I am a dry tree."**
4. **For this is what God says to eunuchs: "To those who observe My Sabbath and choose what pleases Me, and cling to My covenant,**
5. **"I will give them, in My house and inside My fortress walls, an eternal memorial that shall not be [cut off]\exiled, better than sons or daughters.**
6. **"And as for a non-Israelite\[cut-off person] who is connected to and serving God, and loving God's reputation, anyone who observes the Sabbath, not profaning it, and clinging to My covenant,**
7. **"I will bring all of them to My holy mountain and give them joy in My house of prayer. Their burnt-offerings and their sacrifices shall be acceptable on My altar, for My house shall be called a house of prayer for all peoples."**

Amos 5:24*

וְיִגַּל כַּמַּיִם, מִשְׁפָּט; וּצְדָקָה, כְּנַחַל אֵיתָן.

V'-yi-gal ka-ma-yim, mi-sh'-pat; u-ts'-da-ka, k'-na-khal ay-tan.

May justice roll down like water, and righteousness as a secure\unyielding stream.

The verse above from Amos and those from Isaiah on pp. 42-44 above and on pp. 56-57 below express Judaism's traditional universalism that transcends tribalism or nationalism.

---

*Quoted by Martin Luther King in his "Letter from Birmingham Jail."

What Is Holy?

Make something new,
See it cast long, branching shadows
Into the future;
Shape my creation
To cast the most beautiful shadows.

Feel, sense another's suffering and
Madness;
Respectfully whisper to that other
Healing;
Invite that soul to rejoin the universal dance;
Uncover in the madness that person's unique genius.

Look into my darkest, dirtiest places;
Laugh, and turn the darkness into light,
The dirt into luxuriant, blooming, gloriously fertile life.

Hearing the sweet allegretto of a kitten's music,
Play harmonizing riffs
So the kitten climbs onto my lap
And purrs herself to sleep.

Take a child's hand and walk,
Walk,
Sharing the wonder of every moment's newness;
Then, when the child asks,
"What is it like to be old?"
Tell a story that makes the arc of life a rainbow.

Rabbi Abraham Joshua Heschel (1907-1972) said: build your life as if it were a work of art.

commons.wikimedia.org/wiki/File:Double-alaskan-rainbow.jpg
© Eric Rolph at English Wikipedia / Wikimedia Commons / CC-BY-SA-2.5
(http://creativecommons.org/licenses/by-sa/2.5/)

Proverbs 31:10-31

Proverbs 31:10-31 comprise an acrostic poem in which, spanning the entire Hebrew alphabet, successive letters start successive verses. (Other instances in our sacred literature where successive half verses, verses, or groups of verses successively span the alphabet include Psalms 25, 34, 37, 111, 112, and 119; Lamentations 1-4; and the אָשַׁמְנוּ – *a-sha-m'-nu* confessional prayer.) Spanning the alphabet metaphorically implies that the content applies to every possible case.

These Proverbs verses have been recited to celebrate women; they detail the traditional female role. Traditionally, a husband focused on religious study, while his wife not only oversaw childrearing and household management but also ran the family's business or commercial enterprises. Following the first translation below is a second gender-neutral one; it reflects more modern lifestyle, wherein both men and women are celebrated for nonviolent exploits, including business and commerce.

10

אֵשֶׁת־חַיִל, מִי יִמְצָא? וְרָחֹק מִפְּנִינִים מִכְרָהּ.

Ay-shet kha-yil, mee yi-m'-tsa? V'-ra-khok mi-p'-nee-neem mi-kh'-ra.

Who can find a heroic woman? She is worth far more than pearls.

11

בָּטַח בָּהּ, לֵב בַּעְלָהּ וְשָׁלָל לֹא יֶחְסָר.

Ba-takh ba, layv ba-'-la v'-sha-lal lo ye-kh'-sar.

Her husband's heart trusts her, and he will not lack profit.

12

גְּמָלַתְהוּ טוֹב וְלֹא־רָע כֹּל יְמֵי חַיֶּיהָ:

G'-ma-la-t'-hu tov v'-lo ra kol y'-may kha-yay-a:

She repays him with good, and not evil, all the days of her life:

13

דָּרְשָׁה צֶמֶר וּפִשְׁתִּים וַתַּעַשׂ בְּחֵפֶץ כַּפֶּיהָ.

Da-r'-sha tse-mer u-fi-sh'-teem va-ta-as b'-khay-fets ka-pay-a.

She seeks out wool and flax and makes from them what her hands desire.

14

הָיְתָה כָּאֳנִיּוֹת סוֹחֵר: מִמֶּרְחָק תָּבִיא לַחְמָהּ;

Ha-y'-ta ka-a-nee-yot so-khayr: mi-me-r'-khak ta-vee la-kh'-ma ;

She is like a merchant ship: she brings her bread from distant places;

15

וַתָּקָם בְּעוֹד לַיְלָה וַתִּתֵּן טֶרֶף לְבֵיתָהּ וְחֹק לְנַעֲרֹתֶיהָ.

Va-ta-kam b'-od la-y'-la va-ti-tayn te-ref l'-vay-ta v'-khok l'-na-a-ro-tay-a.

While yet night she arises and gives her menage food\prey and her girls orders.

Proverbs 31:10-31 Cont.

16
זָמְמָה שָׂדֶה וַתִּקָּחֵהוּ; מִפְּרִי כַפֶּיהָ נָטְעָ כָּרֶם.
*Za-m'-ma sa-de va-ti-ka-**khay**-hu; mi-p'-ree **kha-pay**-a na-t'-a **ka**-rem.*
She appraises a field and buys it; from her craft's fruit she plants a vineyard.

17
חָגְרָה בְעוֹז מָתְנֶיהָ וַתְּאַמֵּץ זְרוֹעֹתֶיהָ.
*Kha-g'-ra v'-oz ma-t'-**nay**-a va-t'-a-mayts z'-ro-o-**tay**-a.*
She girds her loins with strength and her arms with courage.

18
טָעֲמָה כִּי־טוֹב סַחְרָהּ; לֹא־יִכְבֶּה בַלַּיְלָה נֵרָהּ;
*Ta-a-ma kee tov sa-**kh**'-ra; lo yi-**kh**'-be va-la-y'-la nay-ra;*
She assesses that her business is good; her candle does not go out at night;

19
יָדֶיהָ שִׁלְּחָה בַכִּישׁוֹר, וְכַפֶּיהָ תָּמְכוּ פָלֶךְ.
*Ya-**day**-a shi-l'-**kh**a va-kee-shor, v'-**kha-pay**-a ta-m'-**kh**u **fa**-lekh.*
She extends her hands to the distaff, and her palms grasp a spindle.

20
כַּפָּהּ פָּרְשָׂה לֶעָנִי, וְיָדֶיהָ שִׁלְּחָה לָאֶבְיוֹן.
*Ka-pa pa-r'-sa le-a-nee, v'-ya-**day**-a shi-l'-**kha** la-e-v'-yon.*
She opens her palm to the wretched, and extends her hands to a pauper.

21
לֹא־תִירָא לְבֵיתָהּ מִשָּׁלֶג כִּי כָל־בֵּיתָהּ לָבֻשׁ שָׁנִים;
*Lo tee-ra l'-vay-ta mi-**sha**-leg kee khawl bay-ta la-vush sha-neem;*
For her menage she does not fear snow as all in her household are clad richly.

22
מַרְבַדִּים עָשְׂתָה־לָּהּ; שֵׁשׁ וְאַרְגָּמָן לְבוּשָׁהּ.
Ma-r'-va-deem a-s'-ta la; shaysh v'-a-r'-ga-man l'-vu-sha.
She makes carpets for herself; she is dressed in fine and purple garments.

23
נוֹדָע בַּשְּׁעָרִים בַּעְלָהּ בְּשִׁבְתּוֹ עִם־זִקְנֵי־אָרֶץ.
*No-da ba-sh'-a-reem ba-'-la b'-shi-v'-to im zi-k'-nay **a**-rets.*
Her husband is known in the public forum where he sits with the land's elders.

Proverbs 31:10-31 Cont.

24
סָדִין עָשְׂתָה וַתִּמְכֹּר וַחֲגוֹר נָתְנָה לַכְּנַעֲנִי.
Sa-deen a-s'-ta va-ti-m'-kor va-kha-gor na-t'-na la-k'-na-a-nee.
She makes and sells wraps, and delivers belts to the merchant.

25
עֹז־וְהָדָר לְבוּשָׁהּ, וַתִּשְׂחַק לְיוֹם אַחֲרוֹן.
Oz v'-ha-dar l'-vu-sha, va-ti-s'-khak l'-yom a-kha-ron.
She is dressed in strength and dignity, and she smiles about the future.

26
פִּיהָ פָּתְחָה בְחָכְמָה, וְתוֹרַת־חֶסֶד עַל־לְשׁוֹנָהּ.
Pee-a pa-t'-kha v'-kha-kh'-ma, v'-to-rat khe-sed al l'-sho-na.
She opens her mouth wisely, and the law of lovingkindness is on her tongue.

27
צוֹפִיָּה הֲלִיכוֹת בֵּיתָהּ, וְלֶחֶם עַצְלוּת לֹא תֹאכֵל.
Tso-fi-ya ha-lee-khot bay-ta, v'-le-khem a-ts'-lut lo to-khayl.
She checks on the ways of her menage, and does not eat the bread of idleness.

28
קָמוּ בָנֶיהָ וַיְאַשְּׁרוּהָ, בַּעְלָהּ וַיְהַלְלָהּ:
Ka-mu va-nay-a va-y'-a-sh'-ru-a, ba-'la va-y'-ha-l'-la:
Her children rise up and bless her, and her husband praises her:

29
"רַבּוֹת בָּנוֹת עָשׂוּ חָיִל, וְאַתְּ עָלִית עַל־כֻּלָּנָה.
"Ra-bot ba-not a-su kha-yil, v'-at a-leet al-ku-la-na.
"Many daughters have achieved heroically, and you have surpassed them all.

30
"שֶׁקֶר הַחֵן, וְהֶבֶל הַיֹּפִי; אִשָּׁה יִרְאַת־יְיָ, הִיא תִּתְהַלָּל.
"She-ker ha-khayn, v'-he-vel ha-yo-fee; i-sha yi-r'-at A-do-nai, hee ti-t'-ha-lal.
"Grace can fool, and beauty is empty; a woman who fears God shall be praised.

31
"תְּנוּ־לָהּ מִפְּרִי יָדֶיהָ, וִיהַלְלוּהָ בַשְּׁעָרִים מַעֲשֶׂיהָ."
"T'-nu la mi-p'-ree ya-day-a, vee-ha-l'-lu-a va-sh'-a-reem ma-a-say-a."
"Give her of the fruit of her hands, and her works will praise her in the gates."

Proverbs 31:10-31 Cont.

Who can find a staunch marriage partner? Such a one is worth far more than gems,
Inspiring wholehearted trust in her or his spouse, who never lacks benefits.
That marriage partner lifelong returns good, not evil, to his or her spouse:
Seeks out raw materials, and from them creates objects of beauty and value;
Like a merchant ship, brings goods from afar;
Gets up before dawn to provide for the menage and direct the staff;
Appraises and invests wisely, and for growth reinvests the returns.
With hardihood and resolve,
Assessing her or his projects, that they flourish, devoting to them a full day's work,
Skillfully using whatever tools are most appropriate.
Generous and charitable to the needy,
Makes appropriate provision for dealing with possible misfortunes or challenges,
Caring for him- or herself, presenting an image of prosperity and worth.
Consequently, that person's spouse is esteemed among the nation's leaders.
That person produces and markets sought-after goods,
And, dressed in strength and dignity, smiles confidently about the future,
Speaking wisely and with kindness.
That person manages her or his menage with diligence, frugality, industry, and skill.
That person's dependents are grateful, and that person's spouse praises:
"Many have accomplished much, but you have surpassed them all;
"You earn praise for your God-respecting ways, not merely for shallow facade.
"May you benefit from your work, and your accomplishments decide your reputation."

Ecclesiastes Rabbah (Haggadic Commentary) 7:13

When God created the first humans, He showed them all the Garden of Eden's greenery, and said: "Look at My works! See how beautiful and perfect they are! I created them for you. Take care not to spoil or ruin My universe, for if you do, there will be no one after you to repair it."

Rabbi Zalman Meshullam Schachter-Shalomi (1924-2014), a founder of the Jewish Renewal movement, proposed that the laws of kashruth be extended to take into account the environmental, social, and ethical contexts in which food is produced and consumed. This extension, known as "eco-kashruth," has come to be accepted by many. To be eco-kosher, food must be sustainably produced and consumed. For example, an otherwise kosher meal may not be eco-kosher, i.e., be eco-trayf, if it is served on plastic dishes that will take centuries to decompose. Unhealthy or exploitive working conditions of those who labor to produce food or bring it to the consumer may also render it eco-trayf, and so may producing or distributing it in ways that waste non-renewable energy or contribute to undesirable climate change.

Eco-kashruth is in the spirit of some Biblical commandments about food, such as the commandment in Leviticus 23:22 that forbids reaping in a corner of a field: that produce is reserved for the poor; for anyone else it is trayf.

After the *A-mee-da* (Standing) Prayer and Meditation

CONGREGANTS: PLEASE RECITE TOGETHER:

Psalm 19:15

יִהְיוּ לְרָצוֹן אִמְרֵי־פִי וְהֶגְיוֹן לִבִּי, לְפָנֶיךָ, יְיָ צוּרִי וְגֹאֲלִי:

Yi-h'-yu l'-ra-tson i-m'-ray fee v'-he-g'-yon li-bee l'-fa-**nay**-kha, A-don-ai tsu-ree v'-go-a-lee.

May the words of my mouth and the reasoning of my heart be according to Your will, God, my Stronghold and my Redeemer.

May what I say and what I think or feel be what You desire, God, my Bastion and my Redeemer.

E-lo-hai,	אֱלֹהַי,
n'-tsor l'-sho-nee may-ra,	נְצוֹר לְשׁוֹנִי מֵרָע.
u-s'-fa-tai mi-da-bayr mi-r'-ma,	וּשְׂפָתַי מִדַּבֵּר מִרְמָה:
v'-li-m'-ka-l'-lai na-f'-shee ti-dom.	וְלִמְקַלְלַי נַפְשִׁי תִדּוֹם.

**My God,
guard my tongue from wickedness
and my lips from speaking deceitfully,
and toward those who curse me may my soul be silent.**

May what I say not increase evil in the world, whether by tempting others to behave wickedly or by misleading them with untruths; may I respond without aggression when others say bad things about me or wish I experience misfortune.

O-se Sha-lom

CONGREGANTS: PLEASE SING TOGETHER (THE WORDS IN BRACKETS MAY BE OMITTED):

עֹשֶׂה שָׁלוֹם בִּמְרוֹמָיו הוּא יַעֲשֶׂה שָׁלוֹם עָלֵינוּ וְעַל־כָּל־יִשְׂרָאֵל.
{וְעַל־כָּל־הָעוֹלָם} וְאִמְרוּ אָמֵן:

O-se sha-lom bi-m'-ro-maiv hu ya-a-se sha-lom a-**lay**-nu v'-al kawl yi-s'-ra-ayl
{v'-al kawl ha-olam} V'-i-m'-ru a-mayn.

May the One Who makes peace in the high heavens make peace for us and for all Israel {and for all the world}. And let us say "Amen."

May the peace that reigns in the high heavens descend on us, on all Israel, and on all the world.

The Soul Is Pure

אֱלֹהַי, נְשָׁמָה שֶׁנָּתַתָּ בִּי טְהוֹרָה הִיא.

E-lo-hai, n'-sha-ma she-na-ta-ta bee t'-ho-ra hee.

My God, the soul You placed in me is pure.

It Is Up To Us

CONGREGANTS: PLEASE RISE.

עָלֵינוּ לְשַׁבֵּחַ לַאֲדוֹן הַכֹּל, לָתֵת גְּדֻלָּה לְיוֹצֵר בְּרֵאשִׁית,
שֶׁהוּא שָׂם חֶלְקֵנוּ לְיַחֵד אֶת־שְׁמוֹ.
וְגוֹרָלֵנוּ לְהַמְלִיךְ מַלְכוּתוֹ.*
רֹקַע הָאָרֶץ וְצֶאֱצָאֶיהָ נָתַן נְשָׁמָה לָעָם עָלֶיהָ וְרוּחַ לַהֹלְכִים בָּהּ:
וַאֲנַחְנוּ כֹּרְעִים וּמִשְׁתַּחֲוִים וּמוֹדִים לִפְנֵי מֶלֶךְ מַלְכֵי הַמְּלָכִים, הַקָּדוֹשׁ בָּרוּךְ הוּא

*A-**lay**-nu l'-sha-**bay**-akh la-a-don ha-kol, la-tayt g'-du-la l'-yo-tsayr b'-ray-sheet,*
*she-Hu sam khe-l'-**kay**-nu l'-ya-khayd et sh'-mo,*
*v'-go-ra-**lay**-nu l'-ha-m'-leekh ma-l'-khu-to.*
*Ro-ka ha-a-rets v'-tse-e-tsa-**ay**-a no-tayn n'-sha-ma la-am a-**lay**-a v'-**ru**-akh la-ho-l'-kheem ba.*
*Va-a-**na**-kh'-nu ko-r'-eem u-mi-sh'-ta-kha-veem u-mo-deem li-f'-nay **me**-lekh ma-l'-khay ha-m'-la-kheem, ha-Ka-dosh ba-rukh Hu.*

It is up to us to celebrate the Master\Mistress of everything, to ascribe greatness to the One Who brought forth in the beginning,
for God made it our destiny to unify God's reputation,
and our role to declare God the sovereign of God's domain.
God provided the background for the earth and its offspring, gave people on it a soul, and breath\spirit to those who walk upon it.
And we kneel and bow and are grateful, before the Sovereign, Ruler of rulers, the Holy One, Who is blessed.

God gave people awareness, gave life to those who walk the earth, and created the backdrop for the earthly experiences of those who have blossomed on this world.
And we bow gratefully, acknowledging that God's sovereignty transcends any human monarch's.

CONGREGANTS: YOU MAY BE SEATED.

---

*The Hebrew text here is based partly on that in *Gates of Prayer*, 4th Printing 1977, © 1975, Central Conference of American Rabbis, and partly on that in *Kol ha-n'-sha-ma* [**Voice of the Spirit**] Second Edition, The Reconstructionist Press, Elkins Park, PA: 2002, © 1996, The Reconstructionist Press.

It Is Up To Us Cont.

עַל־כֵּן נְקַוֶּה לְּךָ, יְיָ אֱלֹהֵינוּ, לִרְאוֹת מְהֵרָה בְּתִפְאֶֽרֶת עֻזֶּֽךָ,
לְהַעֲבִיר גִּלּוּלִים מִן הָאָֽרֶץ, וְהָאֱלִילִים כָּרוֹת יִכָּרֵתוּן,
לְתַקֵּן עוֹלָם בְּמַלְכוּת שַׁדַּי, וְכָל־בְּנֵי בָשָׂר יִקְרְאוּ בִשְׁמֶֽךָ,
לְהַפְנוֹת אֵלֶֽיךָ כָּל־רִשְׁעֵי אָֽרֶץ.

Al kayn n'-ka-ve l'-kha, A-do-nai E-lo-hay-nu, li-r'-ot m'-hay-ra b'-ti-f'-e-ret u-ze-kha,
l'-ha-a-veer gi-lu-leem min ha-a-rets, v'-ha-e-lee-leem ka-rot yi-ka-ray-tun,
l'-ta-kayn o-lam b'-ma-l'-khut sha-dai, v'-khawl b'-nay va-sar yi-k'-r'-u vi-sh'-me-kha,
l'-ha-f'-not ay-lay-kha kawl ri-sh'-ay a-rets.

Accordingly, our hope is directed toward You, our divine God, to behold soon the splendor of Your power,
the transference of idols out of the world, and utter mowing down of false gods,
by the sovereignty of the Almighty bringing about the normalizing of the universe, and all the children of flesh shall call upon Your name,
and turn toward You all the land's wicked ones.

Because You exist, God, we are hopeful. Your plan's fruition is a beautiful drama we look forward to: Only You will be considered flawless, and never will fidelity to a doctrine, cause, organization, tribe, or human-made or natural object be the excuse for cruelty or immorality. Thus, we will join you in remedying all injustice and imperfection, as all humankind, even those presently wicked, turn toward You and call upon You.

יַכִּֽירוּ וְיֵדְעוּ כָּל־יוֹשְׁבֵי תֵבֵל כִּי לְךָ תִּכְרַע כָּל־בֶּֽרֶךְ,
תִּשָּׁבַע כָּל־לָשׁוֹן.
בַּיּוֹם הַהוּא יִהְיֶה יְיָ אֶחָד וּשְׁמוֹ אֶחָד.

Ya-kee-ru v'-yay-d'-u kawl yo-sh'-vay tay-vayl kee l'-kha ti-kh'-ra kawl be-rekh,
ti-sha-va kawl la-shon.
Ba-yom ha-hu yee-h'-ye A-do-nai e-khad u-sh'-mo e-khad.

All who dwell in the world will realize and know that to You every knee should bend, by You every tongue should pledge.
In that day God will be one and God's name will be one.

And it has been foretold: "God shall rule over all lands."
We will fully in the depths of our beings grasp and be possessed by the understanding and insight that to You we should pledge loyalty in word and action.
When that time comes, all humankind will agree about God's nature and will speak of God in the same way.

It Is Up To Us Cont.

Some Orthodox authorities maintain that Joshua originated this prayer after the fall of Jericho.

The *A-lay-nu* has been interpreted to assert that only the Jews are a chosen people with a unique destiny. However, we recognize that every people, like every individual, has a unique destiny and, therefore, in some way is specially chosen. The *A-lay-nu* also declares the ultimate sovereignty of Divine and moral forces over our lives. As we recite it, we express the hope that some day all humanity will be united under a single moral law, one voluntarily accepted, not coercively imposed. Judaism's prophets proclaimed that rulers and masters are subject to the same moral law as their subordinates. Historian of culture Friedrich Nietzsche wrote that moral law does not come from God. Nazi and fascist interpreters of Nietzsche have claimed he felt that different moral laws apply to superiors and subordinates, and superiors have a right to be cruel to their inferiors.

It is remarkable that traditionally we consider it our task or duty to pray to, or praise or celebrate God. Can our doing so matter? Perhaps it does because it –
- improves a person who does so,
- improves those who observe us doing so, and
- when communal, favors bonding among those who participate.

Perhaps God desires all this.

Rabbi Abraham Joshua Heschel stated that in Jewish tradition the primary purpose of prayer is not to make requests; rather, it is to praise, to sing, or to chant, because prayer's essence is song, and we cannot live without song. Though prayer may not save us, it may make us worthy of being saved. He also maintained that prayer should be subversive, should seek to overthrow and ruin the pyramids of callousness, falsehood, hatred, and opportunism.

The sages and prophets longed for the messianic era, not so that then they might be venerated or rule the heathens or even rule the whole world, or that they might eat, drink, and be merry, but rather that undisturbed and safe from oppression they might devote themselves to studying sacred writings and acquiring wisdom.
Mishneh Torah, Hilkhot Melakheem – Review of Torah, Laws of Kings 12:4 – Maimonides

Isaiah 2:4

לֹא יִשָּׂא גוֹי אֶל גוֹי חֶרֶב,
וְלֹא־יִלְמְדוּ עוֹד מִלְחָמָה.

*Lo yi–sa goy el goy **khe**-rev,*
*V'-lo yi-l'-m'–du od mi-l'-**kha**-ma.*

A nation shall not raise a sword against a nation,
Nor shall they study warfare ever again.

Missiles from land to land won't soar
Nor will lands learn the ways of war.

* * * * * * * * * *

I'm gonna lay down my sword and shield
Down by the riverside.
I ain't gonna study war no more.

http://commons.wikimedia.org/wiki/File:Peace-3langs.svg Public Domain

One may not make war against any people until first having offered them peace.
Mishneh Torah, Hilkhot Melakheem – Review of Torah, Laws of Kings 6:1 – Maimonides

Exodus 23:2 commands: "Do not follow the crowd to do wrong." This commandment may imply that doing popular wrong is worse than doing idiosyncratic wrong. Recently, weapons of war have become so powerful they could exterminate all life on our planet. Is war our time's outstanding popular wrong?

Isaiah 2:4 Cont.

Our ancestors suffered. But no one's ancestors were free of suffering. Where in the world today is there no suffering? Who alive today has been or is immune to suffering?

Many carry backbreaking and heart-hardening sacks yoked across their aching shoulders, stuffed to overflowing with desiccated relics of time-worn agonies, sometimes many generations old. Those sacks' moldering contents are fertilizer wherein grow hackneyed but fierce hatreds, stale but powerful grudges. And many backs are bowed by today's pains' crushing burdens, or stoop under dread of future suffering.

Let us lighten our loads: let us rip open those sacks crammed with relics of ancient wrongs. Let us dissolve their dusty contents in reconciliatory tears, or blow them away with gusts of forgiving laughter. Let us replace revengefulness with forgiveness. Let us stop reliving suffering, ancient or modern. Let us stop anticipating future abuse we may never experience.

May we see through whatever hideous masks our imaginations paste over the faces of those we blame for our pain, those we label our enemies. Those masks often cover human faces like ours suffering and fearful . Let us realize that others may be tempted to hurt us because they blame us for their pain, or fear we may hurt them, just as we may be tempted to mistreat others by our belief that they mistreat or have mistreated or may mistreat us.

Abuse does not give the abused license to recycle abuse.

As we yearn for freedom from suffering, as we long for surcease, let us wish that the selfsame yearning be fulfilled for all, the same peace achieved. May our hearts be softened by our well-wishing for others. As we wish our broken hearts and bent backs be healed, let us wish healing for all.

Memorial (Mourning) Meditation

Psalm 144:3-4

יְיָ, מָה־אָדָם, וַתֵּדָעֵהוּ, בֶּן־אֱנוֹשׁ, וַתְּחַשְּׁבֵהוּ. אָדָם, לַהֶבֶל דָּמָה; יָמָיו, כְּצֵל עוֹבֵר:

*A-do-nai, ma a-dam, va-tay-da-**ay**-hu: ben e-nosh, va-t'-**kha**-sh'-**vay**-hu. A-dam, la-**he**-vel da-ma; ya-maiv, k'-tsayl o-vayr:*

God, what is a human, to whom You attend, offspring of a mortal, whom You consider; a human is like mist, whose days are like a passing shadow.

Eternal God, compared to You we are fleetingly evanescent, like vapor, like transient shadows; we are awestruck that You even notice us.

Psalm 90:6

בַּבֹּקֶר יָצִיץ וְחָלָף לָעֶרֶב יְמוֹלֵל וְיָבֵשׁ:

*Ba-**bo**-ker ya-tseets v'-kha-laf la-**e**-rev y'-mo-layl v'-ya-vaysh:*

Blossoming in the morning and by evening passing away withered and dried up:

Like day flowers, though in our mornings we spring up blossoming, by evening we are withered and dried.

Psalm 90:12

לִמְנוֹת יָמֵינוּ כֵּן הוֹדַע וְנָבִא לְבַב חָכְמָה:

*Li-m'-not ya-**may**-nu kayn ho-da v'-na-vi l'-vav kha-**kh**'-ma:*

Teach us to count our days so as to have insightfully and presciently a wise heart:

May realizing how few our days are, and how inevitable their end is, teach us wisdom in heart and mind.

The Mourners' Kaddish

THOSE WHO WILL RECITE THE KADDISH, PLEASE STAND.

יִתְגַּדַּל וְיִתְקַדַּשׁ שְׁמֵהּ רַבָּה. בְּעָלְמָא דִּי־בְרָא כִרְעוּתֵהּ. וְיַמְלִיךְ מַלְכוּתֵהּ. בְּחַיֵּיכוֹן וּבְיוֹמֵיכוֹן. וּבְחַיֵּי דְכָל־בֵּית יִשְׂרָאֵל. בַּעֲגָלָא וּבִזְמַן קָרִיב. וְאִמְרוּ אָמֵן:*

Yi-t'-ga-dal v'-yi-t'-ka-dash sh-may ra-ba. B'-a-l'-ma dee v'-ra khi-r'-u-tay. V'-ya-m'-leekh ma-l'-khu-tay.
B'-kha-yay-khon u-v'-yo-may-khon. U-v'-kha-yay d'-khawl bayt Yi-s'-ra-ayl. Ba-a-ga-la u-vi-z'-man ka-reev. V'-i-m'-ru a-mayn.*

May God's transcendent\great name\reputation be magnified and sanctified in the\this world\universe that was created according to God's will\nurturing\friendship. And may God's sovereignty reign

in your lifetime and in your days and in the lives of all the house of Israel [as in a wheeled vehicle]\expeditiously and in a brief time. And let us say, "Amen."

ALL SAY:

יְהֵא שְׁמֵהּ רַבָּא מְבָרַךְ. לְעָלַם וּלְעָלְמֵי עָלְמַיָּא:

Y'-hay sh'-may ra-ba m'-va-rakh. L'-a-lam u-l'-a-l'-may a-l'-ma-ya.

May God's transcendent\great name\reputation be blessed universally in space and time and to the ultimate reaches of time and space of the\this world\universe.

KADDISH RECITERS CONTINUE:

יִתְבָּרַךְ. וְיִשְׁתַּבַּח. וְיִתְפָּאַר. וְיִתְרוֹמַם. וְיִתְנַשֵּׂא. וְיִתְהַדָּר. וְיִתְעַלֶּה. וְיִתְהַלָּל. שְׁמֵהּ דְּקֻדְשָׁא

Yi-t'-ba–rakh. V'-yi-sh'-ta-bakh. V'-yi-t'-pa-ar. V'-yi-t'-ro-mam. V'-yi-t'-na-say. V'-yi-t'-ha-dar. V'-yi-t'-a-le. V'-yi-t'-ha-lal. Sh'-may d'-Ku-d'-sha

May be blessed and thanked and elevated and glorified and raised up and lifted up and boosted and praised the name\reputation of the Holy One.

ALL SAY:

בְּרִיךְ הוּא.

B'-reekh Hu.

On Whom, blessings.

---

*In Hebrew, אמן is an acronym for "God is a faithful sovereign."

The Mourners' Kaddish Cont.

KADDISH RECITERS CONTINUE:

לְעֵלָּא לְעֵלָּא* מִן־כָּל**־בִּרְכָתָא. וְשִׁירָתָא. תֻּשְׁבְּחָתָא. וְנֶחֱמָתָא. דַּאֲמִירָן בְּעָלְמָא. וְאִמְרוּ אָמֵן:

יְהֵא שְׁלָמָא רַבָּא מִן־שְׁמַיָּא. וְחַיִּים. עָלֵינוּ וְעַל־כָּל־יִשְׂרָאֵל {וְעַל־כָּל־גּוֹיֵי־הָאָרֶץ.} וְאִמְרוּ אָמֵן:

עוֹשֶׂה שָׁלוֹם בִּמְרוֹמָיו. הוּא יַעֲשֶׂה שָׁלוֹם. עָלֵינוּ וְעַל־כָּל־יִשְׂרָאֵל. {וְעַל־כָּל־גּוֹיֵי־הָאָרֶץ.} וְאִמְרוּ אָמֵן:

L'-**ay**-la l'-**ay**-la* min kawl** bi-r'-<u>kha</u>-ta. V'-shee-ra-ta. Tu-sh'-b'-<u>kha</u>-ta. V'-ne-<u>khe</u>-ma-ta. Da-a-mee-ran b'-a-l'-ma. V'-i-m'-ru a-mayn.

Y'-hay sh'-la-ma ra-ba min sh'-ma-ya. V'-<u>kha</u>-yeem a-**lay**-nu v'-al kawl Yi-s'-ra-ayl. {V'-al kawl go-yay ha-**a**-rets.} V'-i-m'-ru a-mayn.

O-se sha-lom bi-m'-ro-maiv. Hu ya-a-se sha-lom. A-**lay**-nu v'-al kawl Yi-s'-ra-ayl. {V'-al kawl go-yay ha-**a**-rets.} V'-i-m'-ru a-mayn.

Transcending beyond* all blessings and psalms, praises and consolations that are uttered in the world. And let us say, "Amen."

May there be abundant peace from heaven. And life for us and for all Israel. {And for all the nations of the earth.} And let us say, "Amen."

May the One Who makes peace in the celestial spheres make peace for us and for all Israel. {And for all the nations of the earth.} And let us say, "Amen."

---

*Said traditionally on the Sabbath

**On the Sabbath before Yom Kippur מִכָּל [mi-kawl] is traditionally substituted.

The Mourners' Kaddish Cont.

The Mourners' Kaddish, traditionally referred to as "The Orphan's Prayer," is one of several similar Kaddishes that derive from a prayer that in classical times marked the end of a rabbinic discourse and now mark the ends of sections of a prayer service. Nowadays, it is traditionally recited by mourners participating in a congregational service during the first eleven months following the death of a person mourned, and on each anniversary of the death. In contemporary Israel, customarily everyone recites it on the Tenth of Tevet. Two millennia ago, the rabbis wanted to ensure that those who said a Kaddish would understand it. Therefore, unlike most of the rest of the traditional prayer service, a Kaddish, except for its last stanza (which quotes Job 25:2), is not in Hebrew. It is in Aramaic, the street language of Jews in those times. The Mourners' Kaddish, one might expect, would express grief and sense of loss. However, it is a ringing affirmation of confidence in the power and goodness of God. In effect, the mourners proclaim that, even in a time of loss, their faith is unshaken. Some of its words' meanings have changed. My translation strives to reflect what the Kaddish might mean to a contemporary speaker of its language.

We stand when we recite the Kaddish to –

- commemorate relatives or friends,
- express solidarity with others who are standing,
- commemorate the victims of the Holocaust,
- commemorate those for whom no one else stands,
- commemorate those in the distant or recent past who have been forgotten, so that none are completely forgotten,
- remind ourselves that we are part of a chain of living that stretches from the distant forgotten past to the distant future when we may have been forgotten.

Nothing Is Like Our God

*Ayn k*Ay-lo-**hay**-nu,	אֵין כֵּאלֹהֵינוּ,
*Ayn k*A-do-**nay**-nu,	אֵין כַּאדוֹנֵנוּ,
*Ayn k'-Ma-l'-**kay**-nu,*	אֵין כְּמַלְכֵּנוּ,
*Ayn k'-Mo-shee-**ay**-nu.*	אֵין כְּמוֹשִׁיעֵנוּ.
*Mee kh*Ay-lo-**hay**-nu?	מִי כֵאלֹהֵינוּ?
*Mee kh*A-do-**nay**-nu?	מִי כַּאדוֹנֵנוּ?
*Mee kh'-Ma-l'-**kay**-nu?*	מִי כְמַלְכֵּנוּ?
*Mee k'-Mo-shee-**ay**-nu?*	מִי כְּמוֹשִׁיעֵנוּ?
*No-de l*Ay-lo-**hay**-nu,	נוֹדֶה לֵאלֹהֵינוּ,
*No-de l*A-do-**nay**-nu,	נוֹדֶה לַאדוֹנֵנוּ,
*No-de l'-Ma-l'-**kay**-nu,*	נוֹדֶה לְמַלְכֵּנוּ,
*No-de l'-Mo-shee-**ay**-nu.*	נוֹדֶה לְמוֹשִׁיעֵנוּ.
*Ba-ru**kh** E-lo-**hay**-nu,*	בָּרוּךְ אֱלֹהֵינוּ,
*Ba-ru**kh** A-do-**nay**-nu,*	בָּרוּךְ אֲדוֹנֵנוּ,
*Ba-ru**kh** Ma-l'-**kay**-nu,*	בָּרוּךְ מַלְכֵּנוּ,
*Ba-ru**kh** Mo-shee-**ay**-nu.*	בָּרוּךְ מוֹשִׁיעֵנוּ.
*A-ta hu E-lo-**hay**-nu,*	אַתָּה הוּא אֱלֹהֵינוּ,
*A-ta hu A-do-**nay**-nu,*	אַתָּה הוּא אֲדוֹנֵנוּ,
*A-ta hu Ma-l'-**kay**-nu,*	אַתָּה הוּא מַלְכֵּנוּ,
*A-ta hu Mo-shee-**ay**-nu.*	אַתָּה הוּא מוֹשִׁיעֵנוּ.
*A-ta hu she-hi-k'-**tee**-ru a-vo-**tay**-nu*	אַתָּה הוּא שֶׁהִקְטִירוּ אֲבוֹתֵינוּ
*l'-fa-**nay**-kha et k'-**to**-ret ha-sa-meem.*	לְפָנֶיךָ אֶת קְטֹרֶת הַסַּמִּים.

Nothing Is Like Our God Cont.

Nothing is like our God,
Nothing is like our Liege
Nothing is like our Sovereign,
Nothing is like our Liberator.

Who is like our God?
Who is like our Liege?
Who is like our Sovereign?
Who is like our Liberator?

May our God be known,
May our Liege be known,
May our Sovereign be known,
May our Liberator be known.

Blessed is our God,
Blessed is our Liege,
Blessed is our Sovereign,
Blessed is our Liberator.

You are our God,
You are our Liege,
You are our Sovereign,
You are our Liberator.

Before You, our ancestors burned fragrant spices.

Yi-g'-dal

Yi-g'-dal E-lo-heem khai v'-yi-sh'-ta-bakh Ni-m'-tsa v'-ayn ayt el m'-tsee-u-to.	יִגְדַּל אֱלֹהִים חַי וְיִשְׁתַּבַּח נִמְצָא וְאֵין עֵת אֶל מְצִיאוּתוֹ:
E-khad v'-ayn ya-kheed k'-yi-khu-do Ne-'-lam v'-gam ayn sof l'-a-kh'-du-to.	אֶחָד וְאֵין יָחִיד כְּיִחוּדוֹ נֶעְלָם וְגַם אֵין סוֹף לְאַחְדּוּתוֹ:
Ayn lo d'-mut ha-guf v'-ay-no guf Lo na-a-rokh ay-laiv k'-du-sha-to.	אֵין לוֹ דְּמוּת הַגּוּף וְאֵינוֹ גוּף לֹא נַעֲרוֹךְ אֵלָיו קְדֻשָּׁתוֹ:
Ka-d'-mon l'-khawl da-var a-sher ni-v'-ra Ri-shon v'-ayn ray-sheet l'-ray-shee-to.	קַדְמוֹן לְכָל דָּבָר אֲשֶׁר נִבְרָא רִאשׁוֹן וְאֵין רֵאשִׁית לְרֵאשִׁיתוֹ:
Hi-no A-don o-lam l'-khawl no-tsar Yo-re g'-du-la-to u-ma-l'-khu-to.	הִנּוֹ אֲדוֹן עוֹלָם לְכָל נוֹצָר יוֹרֶה גְדֻלָּתוֹ וּמַלְכוּתוֹ:
She-fa n'vu-a-to n'-ta-no El a-n'-shay s'-gu-la-to v'-ti-f'-a-r'-to.	שֶׁפַע נְבוּאָתוֹ נְתָנוֹ אֶל אַנְשֵׁי סְגֻלָּתוֹ וְתִפְאַרְתּוֹ:
Lo kam b'-Yi-s'-ra-ayl k'-Mo-she od Na-vee, u-ma-beet et t'-mu-na-to.	לֹא קָם בְּיִשְׂרָאֵל כְּמֹשֶׁה עוֹד נָבִיא. וּמַבִּיט אֶת תְּמוּנָתוֹ:
To-rat e-met na-tan l'-a-mo Ayl Al yad n'-vee-o ne-e-man bay-to.	תּוֹרַת אֱמֶת נָתַן לְעַמּוֹ אֵל עַל יַד נְבִיאוֹ נֶאֱמַן בֵּיתוֹ:
Lo ya-kha-leef ha-Ayl v'-lo ya-meer da-to L'-o-la-meem l'-zu-la-to.	לֹא יַחֲלִיף הָאֵל וְלֹא יָמִיר דָּתוֹ לְעוֹלָמִים לְזוּלָתוֹ:
Tso-fe v'-yo-**day**-a s'-ta-ray-nu Ma-beet l'-sof da-var b'-ka-d'-ma-to.	צוֹפֶה וְיוֹדֵעַ סְתָרֵינוּ מַבִּיט לְסוֹף דָּבָר בְּקַדְמָתוֹ:
Go-mayl l'-eesh **khe**-sed k'-mi-f'-a-lo No-tayn l'-ra-sha ra k'-ri-sh'-a-to.	גּוֹמֵל לְאִישׁ חֶסֶד כְּמִפְעָלוֹ נוֹתֵן לְרָשָׁע רַע כְּרִשְׁעָתוֹ:
Yi-sh'-lakh l'-kayts ya-meen m'-shee-**kha**-nu Li-f'-dot m'-kha-kay kayts y'-shu-a-to.	יִשְׁלַח לְקֵץ יָמִין מְשִׁיחֵנוּ לִפְדּוֹת מְחַכֵּי קֵץ יְשׁוּעָתוֹ:
May-teem y'-khai-ye Ayl b'-rov kha-s'-do. Ba-rukh a-day ad shaym t'-hi-la-to –	מֵתִים יְחַיֶּה אֵל בְּרֹב חַסְדּוֹ בָּרוּךְ עֲדֵי עַד שֵׁם תְּהִלָּתוֹ:

Blessed forever be God's glorious reputation.

With its rousing traditional melody, this hymn (or *Adon Olam* – see below) often concludes a prayer service. Adding one concluding line, it parallels poetically Maimonides's Thirteen Principles of Faith (see p. 40 above).

A-don O-lam

אֲדוֹן עוֹלָם אֲשֶׁר מָלַךְ בְּטֶרֶם כָּל־יְצִיר נִבְרָא
לְעֵת נַעֲשָׂה בְחֶפְצוֹ כֹּל אֲזַי מֶלֶךְ שְׁמוֹ נִקְרָא:
וְאַחֲרֵי כִּכְלוֹת הַכֹּל לְבַדּוֹ יִמְלֹךְ נוֹרָא
וְהוּא הָיָה וְהוּא הֹוֶה וְהוּא יִהְיֶה בְּתִפְאָרָה:
וְהוּא אֶחָד וְאֵין שֵׁנִי לְהַמְשִׁיל לוֹ לְהַחְבִּירָה
בְּלִי רֵאשִׁית בְּלִי תַכְלִית וְלוֹ הָעֹז וְהַמִּשְׂרָה:
וְהוּא אֵלִי וְחַי גֹּאֲלִי וְצוּר חֶבְלִי בְּעֵת צָרָה
וְהוּ נִסִּי וּמָנוֹס לִי מְנָת כּוֹסִי בְּיוֹם אֶקְרָא
בְּיָדוֹ אַפְקִיד רוּחִי בְּעֵת אִישַׁן וְאָעִירָה
וְעִם־רוּחִי גְוִיָּתִי יְיָ לִי וְלֹא אִירָא:

A-don o-lam a-sher ma-la<u>kh</u>　　　　B'-**te**-rem kawl y'-tseer ni-v'-ra
L'-ayt na-a-sa v'-<u>khe</u>-f'-tso kol　　　　A-zai **me**-le<u>kh</u> sh'-mo ni-k'-ra
V'-a-<u>kh</u>a-ray ki-<u>kh</u>'-lot ha-kol　　　　L'-va-do yi-m'-lo<u>kh</u> no-ra
V'-hu ha-ya v'-hu ho-ve　　　　V'-hu yi-h'-ye b'-ti-f'-a-ra
V'-hu e-<u>kh</u>ad v'-ayn shay-nee　　　　L'-ha-m'-sheel lo l'-ha-<u>kh</u>'-bee-ra
B'-lee ray-sheet b'-lee ta-<u>kh</u>'-leet　　　　V'-lo ha-oz v'-ha-mi-s'-ra
V'-hu ay-lee v'-<u>kh</u>ai **go**-a-lee　　　　V'-tsur <u>kh</u>e-v'-lee b'-ayt tsa-ra
V'-hu ni-see u-ma-nos lee　　　　M'-nat co-see b'-yom e-k'-ra
B'-ya-do a-f'-keed ru-<u>kh</u>ee　　　　B'-ayt ee-shan v'-a-**ee**-ra
V'-im ru-<u>kh</u>ee g'-vi-ya-tee　　　　A-do-nai lee v'-lo ee-ra.

May be by Solomon ibn Gabirol, 1021?-1058?

A-don O-lam Cont.

O Ruler of eternity\the universe\the multiverse Who reigned
Before any creature was created!
When everything was made according to God's desire,
Then Monarch was proclaimed God's name.

And after everything has ended
God alone will reign awesomely;
And God was and is
And will be in splendor.

And God is One, and there is no second
To compare with for companionship.
Without a beginning, without an end,
God has the power and the authority.

And this is my God and my living Savior
And a fortress for my suffering in a time of trouble,
My banner and my refuge,
My cup's portion on a day I cry out.

To God's hand I delegate my spirit
When I sleep and when I awaken,
And with my spirit, also my body.
My God is mine, and I will not fear.

A-don O-lam Cont.

Our God ruled before creation.
   Then all began. When that occurred,
   It was solely by God's word.
As such, it was God's coronation.
	Eternal God, Who reigned supreme
	   Before all living things' creation,
	When all was done the way God willed,
	   Then God was crowned by acclamation.

And after everything is gone,
   Then God will still reign awesomely.
   God was; God is; and God will be
Glorious, though all alone.
	And after all comes to an end,
	   God reigns in awesome isolation;
	And God has been, and God is now,
	   And God will be in coruscation.

And God's unique; there is no other
   To compare, or play God's part.
   With no ending and no start,
God is eminent, with all power.
	And God is One without another
	   To match up with or share relation
	Without a start, without an end,
	   Possessing power and domination.

And God, my living God, redeems.
   My fort in hard times when I suffer.
   God's my banner and my shelter,
My comfort cup for days of screams.
	And God's my God and Savior live,
	   For wounds, my fort and first-aid station;
	And God's my flag and hideaway,
	   My cup of cheer in desperation.

I trust my soul to God's hands' care
   Each time I sleep and wake anew,
   And with my soul, my body, too.
My God's with me. I shall not fear.
	And to God's hand I trust my soul
	   Each time I sleep or I awaken;
	And with my soul, my body, too,
	   God's mine: I feel no trepidation.

The first three stanzas refer to God's cosmic aspect: eternal, omnipotent, and unique. The last two refer to God's intimate, personal aspect as comforter, savior, and trusted support. Above are two efforts to convey the Hebrew poetry in English.

Psalm 23

1. *Mi-z'-mor L'-Da-vid* *A-do-nai ro-ee lo e-kh'-sar:*	א מִזְמוֹר לְדָוִד, יְיָ רֹעִי לֹא אֶחְסָר:
2. *Bi-n'-ot de-she ya-r'-bee-tsay-nee,* *Al may m'-nu-khot y'-na-ha-lay-nee:*	ב בִּנְאוֹת דֶּשֶׁא יַרְבִּיצֵנִי, עַל־מֵי מְנֻחוֹת יְנַהֲלֵנִי:
3. *Na-f'-shee y'-sho-vayv,* *Ya-n'-khay-nee v'-ma-'-g'-lay tse-dek l'-ma-an sh'mo:*	ג נַפְשִׁי יְשׁוֹבֵב, יַנְחֵנִי בְמַעְגְּלֵי־צֶדֶק לְמַעַן שְׁמוֹ:
4. *Gam kee ay-laykh b'-gay tsa-l'-ma-vet, lo ee-ra ra kee A-ta i-ma-dee,* *Shi-v'-t'-kha u-mi-sh'-a-n'-te-kha hay-ma y'-na-kha-mu-nee:*	ד גַּם כִּי־אֵלֵךְ בְּגֵיא צַלְמָוֶת, לֹא־אִירָא רָע כִּי־אַתָּה עִמָּדִי, שִׁבְטְךָ וּמִשְׁעַנְתֶּךָ הֵמָּה יְנַחֲמֻנִי:
5. *Ta-a-rokh l'-fa-nai shu-l'-khan ne-ged tso-r'-rai,* *Di-sha-n'-ta va-she-men ro-shee,* *Ko-see r'-va-ya:*	ה תַּעֲרֹךְ לְפָנַי שֻׁלְחָן נֶגֶד צֹרְרָי, דִּשַּׁנְתָּ בַשֶּׁמֶן רֹאשִׁי, כּוֹסִי רְוָיָה:
6. *Akh tov va-khe-sed yi-r'-d'-fu-nee kawl y'-may kha-yai,* *V'-sha-v'-tee b'-vayt A-do-nai l'-o-rekh ya-meem.*	ו אַךְ טוֹב וָחֶסֶד יִרְדְּפוּנִי כָּל־יְמֵי חַיָּי, וְשַׁבְתִּי בְּבֵית־יְיָ לְאֹרֶךְ יָמִים:

1. A Psalm by David

God is my shepherd; I shall not lack.
2. God makes me lie down in verdant pastures,
leads me to the banks of peaceful waters,
3. restores\[puts back where it belongs] my soul.
In justice circles, [God pardons me]\[I am blessed] for the sake of God's reputation.
4. Also, though I will walk in the gully of death's shadow, I will not be afraid of evil because You are with\beside me.
Your rod\scepter\tribe and Your staff – they will comfort me.
5. You set before me a place-setting opposite my tormentors,
You have annointed my head with oil,
My cup is overflowing.
6. Only goodness and benevolence shall follow me all the days of my life.
And I shall dwell in God's house while days last.

Psalm 23 Cont.

God is my shepherd; I shall not lack.
God makes me lie down in verdant pastures,
leads me to the banks of peaceful waters,
restores my soul.
In justice's court, I am granted God's forgiving mercy for the sake of God's reputation.
Also, as I walk in death's shadowed arroyo, I will not dread evil
because You are with me.
Your rod and Your staff will comfort me.
You have set before me a place-setting in full view of my enemies,
You have annointed my head with fragrant oil,
my cup is overflowing.
Only goodness and benevolence shall follow me all the days of my life,
and I shall reside in God's household as long as time shall last.

This psalm is traditionally sung before the Friday evening Kiddush or at the close of the third Sabbath meal.

commons.wikimedia.org/wiki/File:Rumunia_5806.jpg © Friend of User:Darwinek / Wikimedia Commons / CC-BY-SA-3.0 (http://creativecommons.org/licenses/by-sa/3.0/)

Psalm 23 Cont.

In our increasingly urban culture, where few have cared for or even seen a flock of sheep, and many animals suffer in industrial factory farms, the olden-days relationship between a shepherd and a creature in the shepherd's flock is becoming an obsolete metaphor for God's loving, unselfish nurture of a human. No contemporary relationship suggests an obvious replacement metaphor. The child-parent relationship is different: though parents do often lovingly care for their helpless infants, they may look forward to the baby becoming in time a loving and grateful adult family member. The shepherd can only look forward to a lamb becoming a sheep. Advocates for the ethical treatment of animals, like classical shepherds, do work for animal well-being. However, with the animals for which they advocate, they rarely have the same intimate day-to-day relationship that shepherds have (or had) with members of their flocks. The closest parallel may be the relationship between people and their animal pets.

I am God's well-cared-for pet.
God beds me down on soft cushions.
God provides me a safe, secure nest
where I am refreshed.
No matter what I do, God cherishes me.
Despite my destiny to descend into death's shadowed canyon,
with You beside me, I do not fear misfortune.
Your leash restrains me from straying where I would be unsafe; Your cage keeps me
  protected where I belong.
You set out my food for me where no rival can get it.
Whatever I may want, You provide.
All my life I shall experience only goodness and benevolence,
and I shall live in God's home forever.

"Your rod and Your staff" (or, in the alternative metaphor, "Your leash" and "Your cage") remind us that God's commandments specify not only what we must do but also what we must not do.

Blessing Children

CAREGIVERS (TRADITIONALLY, THE PARENTS OR PARENT SURROGATES) PLACE THEIR HANDS ON EACH CHILD'S HEAD, THEN SAY:

Numbers 6:24-26

יְבָרֶכְךָ יְיָ וְיִשְׁמְרֶךָ:
יָאֵר יְיָ פָּנָיו אֵלֶיךָ וִיחֻנֶּךָ:
יִשָּׂא יְיָ פָּנָיו אֵלֶיךָ וְיָשֵׂם לְךָ שָׁלוֹם:

Y'-va-re-kh'-kha A-do-nai v'-yi-sh'-m'-re-kha.
Ya-ayr A-do-nai pa-naiv ay-**lay**-kha vee-khu-**ne**-kha.
Yi-sa A-do-nai pa-naiv ay-**lay**-kha v'-ya-saym l'-kha sha-lom.

May God bless you and guard you.
May God's face light you and favor you.
May God's intention toward you be favorable.
May God's face uplift toward you and give you peace.
May God approve of you and give you peace.

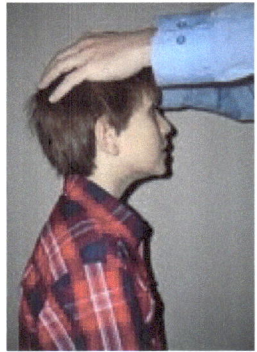

Courtesy Berri Gerjuoy

Traditionally, we highly value family and child-care. This ceremony often takes place at home Friday evening.

Kiddush – Sanctification

commons.wikimedia.org/wiki/File:Shabbat_Candles.jpg © User:Olaf.herfurth / Wikimedia Commons / CC-BY-SA-3.0 (http://creativecommons.org/licenses/by-sa/3.0/)

This Sabbath is the newest link in the great chain of Sabbaths
stretching back to the first Sabbath, the Sabbath of Creation.

We are grateful for this Sabbath, for all Sabbaths,
and for all of Creation:

For the symmetry and luxuriance of flowers
and all else that delights our eyes;

for the rhythm and harmony of music,
the sweet song of birds, the happy prattle of babies,
and all else that delights our ears;

for all things soft and luscious to our touch;

all delightful scents – perfumes and incense;
all delicious tastes, and for all food and drink that sustains us.

Your generosity in having created so much good for us
is the example that reminds us to offer goodness to others.

We celebrate Your goodness to us,
our good fortune in benefitting by Your generosity,
and, filled with thankfulness, we thank You again
for all Your blessings,
and particularly now
for the fruit of the vine,
and for this Sabbath that we hereby sanctify,
Amen.

Kiddush Cup*

---

*commons.wikimedia.org/wiki/File:Kiddush_cup_jerusalem.jpg © User:Ivorymammoth at the English language Wikipedia/ Original author: Dimitri / CC-BY-SA-3.0 (http://creativecommons.org/licenses/by-sa/3.0/) / GFDL (http://en.wikipedia.org/wiki/Wikipedia:Text_of_the_GNU_Free_Documentation_License)

Blessing for Wine

בָּרוּךְ אַתָּה, יְיָ אֱלֹהֵינוּ, מֶלֶךְ הָעוֹלָם, בּוֹרֵא פְּרִי הַגָּפֶן:

*Ba-rukh A-ta, A-do-nai E-lo-**hay**-nu, **me**-lekh ha-o-lam, bo-ray p'-ree ha-**ga**-fen.*

Bless You, [Eternal One]\[Who was, is, and will be], our God, Ruler of the world\universe\multiverse, Who creates the fruit of the vine.

בָּרוּךְ אַתָּה, יְיָ אֱלֹהֵינוּ, מֶלֶךְ הָעוֹלָם,
אֲשֶׁר קִדְּשָׁנוּ בְּמִצְוֹתָיו וְרָצָה בָנוּ.
וְשַׁבַּת קָדְשׁוֹ בְּאַהֲבָה וּבְרָצוֹן הִנְחִילָנוּ זִכָּרוֹן לְמַעֲשֵׂה בְרֵאשִׁית.
כִּי הוּא יוֹם תְּחִלָּה לְמִקְרָאֵי קֹדֶשׁ זֵכֶר לִיצִיאַת מִצְרָיִם.
כִּי־בָנוּ בָחַרְתָּ וְאוֹתָנוּ קִדַּשְׁתָּ מִכָּל־הָעַמִּים וְשַׁבַּת קָדְשְׁךָ בְּאַהֲבָה וּבְרָצוֹן הִנְחַלְתָּנוּ.
בָּרוּךְ אַתָּה, יְיָ, מְקַדֵּשׁ הַשַּׁבָּת:

*Ba-rukh A-ta, A-do-nai E-lo-**hay**-nu, **me**-lekh ha-o-lam,*
*a-sher ki-d'-**sha**-nu b' mi-ts'-vo-taiv v'-**ra**-tsa va-nu,*
*v'-sha-bat ka-d'-sho b'-a-ha-va u-v'-ra-tson hi-n'-**khee-la**-nu zi-ka-ron l'-ma-a-say v'-ray-sheet.*
*Kee hu yom t'-**khi**-la l'-mi-k'-ra-ay **ko**-desh **zay**-kher lee-tsee-at mi-ts'-**ra**-yim.*
*Kee **va**-nu va-**kha**-r'-ta v'-o-**ta**-nu ki-**da**-sh'-ta mi-kawl ha-a-meem v-sha-bat ka-d'-sh'-**kha** b'-a-ha-va u-v'-ra-tson hi-n'-**kha**-l'-**ta**-nu.*
Ba-rukh A-ta, A-do-nai, m'-ka-daysh ha-sha-bat.

Bless You, [Eternal One]\[Who was, is, and will be], our God, Ruler of the world\universe\multiverse
Whose commandments have made us holy and was pleased with us,
and bequeathed to us Your holy Sabbath with love and good will as a memorial of the work of creation.
For it is the first of the sacred days recalling the exodus from Egypt.
For from all the peoples You chose us and made us holy, and bequeathed to us with love and good will Your holy Sabbath.
Bless You, God, Who makes the Sabbath holy.

Historical context elucidates the text above: Today, most peoples have a weekly day of rest; however, two millennia ago Sabbath observance by the Hebrews was exceptional.

Blessing for Bread

בָּרוּךְ אַתָּה, יְיָ אֱלֹהֵינוּ, מֶלֶךְ הָעוֹלָם, הַמוֹצִיא לֶחֶם מִן-הָאָרֶץ:

Ba-rukh A-ta, A-do-nai E-lo-hay-nu, me-lekh ha-o-lam, ha-mo-tsee le-khem min ha-a-rets.

Bless You, [Eternal One]\[Who was, is, and will be], our God, Ruler of the world\universe\multiverse, Who brings forth bread from the earth.

It is noteworthy that the Hebrew word for "war," מלחמה, means literally "lack of bread."

These challahs recall our interdependence, our sharing of values and commitments.

commons.wikimedia.org/wiki/File:Shabbat_Challos.jpg / Public Domain

Ha-sh'-kee-vay-nu

הַשְׁכִּיבֵנוּ יְיָ אֱלֹהֵינוּ לְשָׁלוֹם וְהַעֲמִידֵנוּ שׁוֹמְרֵנוּ לְחַיִּים טוֹבִים.
וּפְרוֹשׂ עָלֵינוּ סֻכַּת שְׁלוֹמֶךָ וְתַקְּנֵנוּ בְּעֵצָה טוֹבָה מִלְּפָנֶיךָ וְהוֹשִׁיעֵנוּ לְמַעַן שְׁמֶךָ.
וּבְצֵל כְּנָפֶיךָ תַּסְתִּירֵנוּ, כִּי אֵל שׁוֹמְרֵנוּ וּמַצִּילֵנוּ, חַנּוּן וְרַחוּם אָתָּה.
וּשְׁמוֹר צֵאתֵנוּ וּבוֹאֵנוּ לְחַיִּים וּלְשָׁלוֹם מֵעַתָּה וְעַד עוֹלָם.
בָּרוּךְ אַתָּה יְיָ הַפּוֹרֵשׂ סֻכַּת שָׁלוֹם עָלֵינוּ וְעַל כָּל יִשְׂרָאֵל וְעַל יְרוּשָׁלָיִם{ וְעַל כָּל הָעוֹלָם}:

*Ha-sh'-kee-**vay**-nu A-do-nai E-lo-**hay**-nu l'-sha-lom v'-ha-a-mee-**day**-nu Sho-m'-ray-nu l'-<u>kha</u>-yeem to-veem.*
*U-f'-ros a-**lay**-nu su-kat sh'-lo-me-<u>kha</u> v'-ta-k'-**nay**-nu b'-ay-tsa to-va mi-l'-fa'-**nay**-<u>kha</u> v'-ho-shee-**ay**-nu l'-**ma**-an sh'-**me**-<u>kha</u>.*
*U-v'-tsayl k'-na-**fay**-<u>kha</u> ta-s'-tee-**ray**-nu, kee Ayl sho-m'-**ray**-nu u-ma-tsee-**lay**-nu, <u>kha</u>-nun v'-ra-<u>kh</u>um A-ta.*
*U-sh'-mor tsay-**tay**-nu u-vo-**ay**-nu l'-<u>kha</u>-yeem u-l'-sha-lom may-a-ta v'-ad o-lam.*
*Ba-ru<u>kh</u> A-ta A-do-nai ha-po-ras su-kat sha-lom a-**lay**-nu v'-al kawl yi-s'-ra-ayl v'-al y'-ru-sha-**la**-yim{ v'-al kawl ha-o-lam}.*

God, lie us down peacefully and raise us up, our Guardian, to a good life.
And spread over us the shelter of Your peace and regulate us with Your good advice and rescue us for the sake of Your reputation.
And in the shade of Your wings may we hide [Psalm 17:8] because You are a God Who guards and rescues us, gracious and merciful [Nehemiah 9:31].
And guard us for life and peace when we leave and when we arrive now and forever [Psalm 121:8].
You are blessed, God, Who spreads the shelter of peace over us and over all Israel, and Jerusalem{, and all the world}.

Ha-sh'-kee-vay-nu Cont.

This prayer is not ordinarily communal. Many observant Jews recite it at bedtime

The Hebrew word for peace, שָׁלוֹם, is linked etymologically and by pronunciation with the Hebrew words for completion and for making a final payment on a debt. Thus, in Hebrew, absence of peace connotes incompleteness and imbalance, like a sequence of notes that ends without resolution on the tonic. Absence of peace also connotes an unfulfilled obligation, hence, an injustice. Through its association with the settling of a debt, absence of peace suggests that someone owes someone, and that therefore attaining peace means moving from a situation where one party has a temporary unfair advantage to a situation where the relations among the parties are balanced. Thus, before peace is achieved, implicitly there is lingering injustice. So, in Hebrew, attaining peace suggests relaxation of tension. It is like assuaging an itch. Moreover, in Hebrew שָׁלוֹם does not connote inactivity; rather, it connotes harmonious activity. The "peace" we see in night's starry dome is the peace of harmonious movement.

commons.wikimedia.org/wiki/File:Hubble_ultra_deep_field_high_rez_edit1.jpg
NASA and the European Space Agency / Modification: Black point adjustment / Public Domain

Acknowledgments

Portions of the present work are based on material its editor composed, edited, or translated for *Kehilat Chaverim*'s *Sabbath Evening Service*, edited by Faith Messer Fuerst, H. G. Gerjuoy, Dorothy Hunt, and Mary Beckoff Williams (Chairperson). I am grateful for helpful comments and suggestions by Ms. Fuerst, Ms. Hunt, and Ms. Williams in connection with our collaboration on *Kehilat Chaverim*'s *Sabbath Evening Service*.

Several persons read successive earlier versions of the present work. I am particularly grateful for thoughtful and helpful critiques, in roughly chronological order, by Rabbi Edward Cohen, Rev. Joanne Choly, Ms. Talya Schenk, and Rabbi James Levinson. Mr. Frank Krasicki made helpful comments about both earlier and more recent versions, and particularly helped clarify my comments about Nietzsche. Ms. Joan Walden offered helpful advice that both included and transcended copy editing. My daughter, Amy Beth Arzuon, was an important source of encouragement. My daughter, Ilana Martha Gerjuoy, provided helpful suggestions and advice. Rabbi Judy Epstein helped give this work an appropriate subtitle. My wife, Carol A. Gerjuoy, has been an ongoing source of much helpful, perceptive advice.

Dr. Donald Pet provided a helpful thoughtful critique that called attention to the inconsistencies implicit in passively depending on God to take care of us and solve our problems for us. He also objected to reducing life's moral complexities to disjunction between non-overlapping distinct "good" and "evil."

I feel special gratitude to Ms. Faith Messer Fuerst, who painstakingly copy edited a recent version of this work, helping me correct many flaws, both minor and major.

My daughter, Berri T. Gerjuoy, did much tedious work finding the sources of and appropriate citations for graphic images.

Joshua Rumbut reminded me that there are intermediate human genders.

Of course, all flaws in the present work are my responsibility; in no way are any persons named above responsible.

www.ingramcontent.com/pod-product-compliance
Lightning Source LLC
Chambersburg PA
CBHW042006150426
43194CB00003B/140